SIX-FIGURE

SALES

SECRETS

The Ultimate Guide to Overfilling Your Pipeline, Closing More, and Earning in the Top 1% of Salespeople

MARCUS CHAN

SIX-FIGURE SALES SECRETS

The Ultimate Guide to Overfilling Your Pipeline, Closing More, and Earning in the Top 1% of Salespeople

For permission requests, speaking inquiries, and bulk order purchase options, email:

support@sixfiguresalesacademy.com

VENLI CONSULTING GROUP LLC
10940 SW BARNES RD. SUITE 193
PORTLAND, OR 97225
venliconsulting.com

eBook ISBN: 979-8-9857704-7-6
Paperback ISBN: 979-8-9857704-6-9

Cover and Interior Design by Transcendent Publishing
www.transcendentpublishing.com

Edited by DragonflyWings.Ink, a division of Lori Lynn Enterprises

Graphics by The Design Desk

Disclaimer: The author makes no guarantees concerning the level of success you may experience by following the advice and strategies contained in this book, and you accept the risk that results will differ for each individual.

You have to learn the rules of the game. And then you have to play better than everyone else.

—Anonymous

CONTENTS

To my parents, who pushed me to be the best version of me, even when I didn't believe in myself.

ADVANCE PRAISE

Marcus is an award-winning seller who has proven himself in the field with distinction. He has the exact profile needed to coach any up-and-coming seller to massive success. He has done it time and again, as evidenced by hundreds of clients who have achieved great results through Marcus' coaching programs. *Six-Figure Sales Secrets* brings all the foundational principles, strategies, and tactics sellers need to get to the next level.

—**Jamal Reimer**, Author of *Mega Deal Secrets*

I've always said that there is one solution to almost every other challenge we face in sales—things like negotiations, discounting, objection-handling, etc.—A BIG FAT PIPELINE. If you know how to prospect effectively and do it consistently, you put yourself in a position where you don't NEED the business, you WANT it. This allows you to sell the right way and for the right reasons with a lot less stress. In this book, Marcus lays out frameworks, techniques, and examples of how to effectively prospect and break through the noise. If you apply the techniques and strategies in this book, you'll never NEED the business again.

—**John Barrows**, CEO of JB Sales

Six-Figure Sales Secrets opens like a Spielberg movie. It hooks you from the start and entertains at a fantastic pace. It's easy to read and more importantly, easy to take action on. A must-read for anyone who wants to grow their sales big time. Sales has changed at a ferocious pace in the last few years, and Marcus Chan shows you how to keep up with the times with insight and tips that work. My favorite sections are talking to the gatekeeper, a breakdown of what to say on a call and voicemail, mental prep and mindset routines to start your day.

—**Niraj Kapur**, LinkedIn Top Sales Voice

Marcus Chan's two decades plus of sales experience speaks for itself. He's packed all of the secrets of the top 1% of salespeople in a book you can read in just a few hours. If you're a sales professional who cares about crushing your quota, you'd be crazy not to buy this right now.

—**Jason Bay**, Founder of Outbound Squad

Marcus is one of the most complete Sales Leaders out there and *Six-Figure Sales Secrets* is the culmination of exactly that. Each chapter contains the perfect blend of stories and actionable insights. This is a must-have for any aspirational seller who strives to become best in class.

—**Alex Alleyne**, Director of Sales, EMEA at
Sales Impact Academy

I've sold over $15M online in the past three years, and this is one of the most comprehensive guides I've seen to take even the most novice salesperson and turn them into a cash-printing machine. I've had the pleasure of having Marcus as a client for almost two years and have seen first-hand the tremendous effects his techniques have on salespeople all over the world, sometimes changing lives in as little as a few weeks. I've always been a fan of "hunting your own game," and Marcus gives you the playbook to do exactly that, allowing you to never worry about where your next deal is coming from again.

—**Ravi Abuvala,** Founder of Scaling with Systems

Six-Figure Sales Secrets is packed with frameworks and tactics that will move the needle of your sales performance and accelerate you toward the top 1% of sales professionals. Marcus masterfully shares how "The Separation Is in the Preparation" and gives the whole blueprint to self source and close six-figure deals. If you plan to exceed 250%+ of your sales target ... this book is a must read!

The best part? It doesn't matter if you're just starting in sales, a seasoned veteran, or even what stage of the financial year it is ... you will discover tips and advice that will help you CLOSE DEALS you're working on RIGHT NOW!

—**Paul M. Caffrey,** Author of *The Work Before the Work: The Hidden Habits Elite Sales Professionals Use to Outperform the Competition*

FOREWORD

The first time I met Marcus, I approached him as a potential competitor on my path to coaching B2B tech sales reps. I had seen him everywhere—on LinkedIn, on YouTube, on Instagram—and I knew he was a credible force in the coaching space, simply because of his presence on all the online channels that I was visiting.

But I was hesitant to reach out because I knew this was a space where I could potentially be competing with him. I had recently decided to pursue coaching full-time, and as a new sales coach, I knew I needed help. I finally reached out and humbly asked Marcus if he had time to meet with me so I could pick his brain and learn about the coaching industry.

He immediately wrote back and agreed to meet with me for 30 minutes. When I met with him, I was absolutely blown away. Not only was he willing to share with me the inside scoop about his business and how he got started but he also shared all of his trials, tribulations, and failures in the beginning.

He showed me the technology he uses. He showed me the team that he has. He showed me his exact business model. He completely opened up transparently and shared precisely what I needed to do to grow my business.

And that's when I knew that Marcus was somebody special who I would continue to keep in touch with for the rest of my life, not only as a mentor but also as a friend.

You see, Marcus approached me the same way that he had been approaching his students and his employees for his entire career. His philosophy is to help other people get what they want—to abundantly serve—and in doing so, he knew that ultimately he would feel joy, contribution, and success from giving back to others.

Since that time, over a year ago, Marcus has continued to mentor me and provide me with insights that I can use to grow my business. We talk every week, and he willingly and openly shares his playbook. We've also had the opportunity to co-present at a sales training for the Salesforce Success Summit, which was an amazing experience.

When Marcus approached me to write this foreword, I was more than happy to oblige because Marcus has given so much to the sales community, and to me personally, that I'm happy to share my thoughts on the book, the person who wrote it, and why it's so valuable for our community.

Before writing this book, Marcus spent over 15 years coaching salespeople on how to succeed from direct, in-the-trenches selling to getting promoted 10X in two highly competitive sales environments. And the crazy part is that he's been wildly successful in every role, winning every possible award, including President's Club. Having come from a similar background to Marcus, where I led sales teams, I can assure you that these accomplishments do not happen until and unless you help other people become successful. And that's exactly what Marcus has done his entire career. He has helped countless people succeed and thrive. Because of that, he's experienced wild success in everything he's ever ventured into with his career, including the writing of this book.

But with the release of *Six-Figure Sales Secrets*, Marcus is now taking everything that he's learned in over 15 years of selling and coaching the world's best salespeople and making it accessible to everybody else. You see, this is the ultimate guide to consistently performing as a top salesperson, and everything that Marcus has laid out is not available in most books.

Many sales books have a lot of fluff and not a lot of meat on the bones, but with *Six-Figure Sales Secrets*, Marcus packs every single page with high-value and actionable frameworks, tactics, and templates that you can use to succeed in sales, regardless of what you sell.

Whether you're new to sales or a seasoned veteran, you'll find that Marcus has put together one guide which has all the fundamentals that have you covered in one simple, easy-to-read, and very actionable sales book. *Six-Figure Sales Secrets* covers every step of the sales stage that you need to be successful, from planning to territory management to prospecting strategies to running a great discovery call to nailing your demo to presenting your proposal and pricing, and finally, to effectively closing, growing, and expanding the accounts that you close. Marcus has it all covered in one place.

Another thing that I love about this book is that it has a big component on personal development. Marcus and I share a belief that when you work hard on your job, you can make a living, but when you work hard on yourself, you can make a fortune. Every day, Marcus shows up, working hard on his body, his mind, and his spirit, so he can perform at his best, and that is something he teaches throughout this book. Marcus shares his morning routine, daily habits, the books that he reads, and all of his secrets to what has made him a successful coach and entrepreneur. As a salesperson, you can apply these habits to grow your own fortune.

I've read many sales books, but very few have as many actionable insights packed on every single page as *Six-Figure Sales Secrets*. This is a proven playbook for success, and given that Marcus has successfully coached thousands of sales reps, taught them the fundamentals of what they need to succeed, and sent countless people to President's Club, you now have the opportunity to learn directly from him. He teaches exactly what it takes to succeed in sales.

I'm honored to call Marcus a friend and a mentor, and I'm grateful that he's written this book to further serve the sales community and complement everything else that he's already given thus far. To get the most out of this book, the key for readers is to apply and practice what Marcus teaches before moving on to the next chapter because everything in this book is actionable and will deliver results.

Marcus is not only a great salesperson, but he's also a great person, and it's my privilege to endorse this book and recommend it to our community. I hope you get as much value from reading *Six-Figure Sales Secrets* as I've received over the past year from having Marcus coach and mentor me.

It's a privilege to work under his leadership and to work alongside him to support the sales community, and I know that this book will help thousands of salespeople learn the fundamentals and set themselves up for successful careers in sales.

—**Ian Koniak**, Founder of Ian Koniak Sales Coaching, Dean of Pavilion's Enterprise Sales School, and Former #1 Enterprise AE at Salesforce

PREFACE

The only real mistake is the one
from which we learn nothing.
—Henry Ford

Most companies use the same recycled sales training over and over.

They tell their employees, "It's a numbers game! Make more calls!"

They offer scripts that sound awkward, making their sales force feel sleazy.

They say that 80-hour work weeks are normal.

Essentially, they expect their sales force to make up for the lack of training by putting in more hours and playing a numbers game with outdated scripts and sales tactics that repel more than they attract.

But not you.

You are about to learn the secrets that only the top 1% of sales experts use (and often don't even know they're using!).

You hold in your hands the key to unlocking a competitive edge that, once you open it, will be the only thing you'll never want to close. (See what I did there?)

You have exactly what you need to master the game of sales.

The trick is to work smarter, not harder.

Stop chasing the numbers and start closing more deals.

Surpass all of your sales goals as you rise to the top of the sales charts, crushing your competition, and becoming the sought-after leader you know you're destined to be.

You have greatness within you.

You were born for more than you're experiencing right now.

And you know it.

You feel it in your bones. At this moment in time, you have done everything you know to do to get to where you are.

What you don't know has been holding you back while your competition races ahead. It's time to not only catch up and join them but also show them how it's done.

Today is the day that you shortcut your way to heights you only dreamed of before.

This book is your unfair advantage to unlock the potential hidden inside you that everyone around you sees but somehow you haven't been able to tap into.

Let the unblocking begin.

SECTION ONE

INTRODUCTION

Every master was once a disaster.
—T. Harv Eker

From Pest Control to President's Club

Joor Bol was a door-to-door sales guy, selling lawn care and pest control. He hit the pavement day in and day out, in rain or sunshine, in freezing cold and blazing heat. He had a difficult background and showed true grit.

He lived in a world where he routinely had to go into rough neighborhoods, walking into at least 300 houses a week, trying to talk strangers into signing a two-year contract for lawn care and pest control.

It was 100% commission, feast or famine. No room for losing. If he didn't sell, he didn't make any money. It was a numbers game. He got up every day to face rejection over and over and over again.

While Joor was out pounding the pavement, I was serving as the new sales leader at a Fortune 500 company, looking to rebuild a sales team. The company I was working for seemed to love hiring a certain profile: 22- to 25-year-old kids who looked like they had just walked out of an Abercrombie & Fitch ad—good-looking, new college grads dressed in a crisp white dress shirt and tie.

Joor didn't fit that mold. Not that he wasn't good-looking, but he wasn't a recent college grad. He was older and rough around the edges. He had never had any true coaching, support, or direction, but I saw a tenacity and fortitude in him. He was my number two hire as I worked to rebuild a winning sales team.

He started working directly for me. Even though he had not had any formal sales training, Joor had raw talent. I started working with him and helped him completely reshift the way he thought and how he worked. He went from being a transactional door-to-door salesman to transforming into a pro at the sales game.

His first year, he made President's Club, which is the top elite award at the company. He broke a ton of records and earned well in the six figures. But on top of that, he did it on his own time frame, working 20 to 30 hours a week.

Time freedom was a dream he had so that he could actually buy his first house, have his first kid, and live the life he always wanted without working 60 to 80 hours a week barely making ends meet.

Fast forward as he continued to work at development and got better and better. He started closing bigger and bigger deals, got promoted multiple times into elite roles, hit President's Club every year, and broke more records.

He became the go-to person that every salesperson in the company wanted to benchmark against. They saw him not only as the expert but also as a person who brought immense value. Because of how effective he was in his sales process, his prospects and customers didn't see him as "just another salesperson." They saw him as an expert authority who could solve their problems.

Now he's earning multiple six figures a year selling to Fortune 500 companies. He lives in his dream house with his wife and two beautiful daughters. He enjoys complete time freedom, which is a nice shift from his long days selling door-to-door. He's wildly happy because now he's earning what he should be earning, while doing what he loves: helping customers solve problems and achieve their goals.

Who Is Marcus Chan?

If we haven't met yet, my name is Marcus Chan. I'm the founder of Venli Consulting Group and Six-Figure Sales Academy. I've generated over $700M in sales contracts over the past decade, I've trained thousands of people, and I've won a bunch of awards like President's Club. But I sure didn't start out this way.

I wasn't born with all the qualities it takes to be a top performer, so I had to learn them the hard way. My parents were Chinese immigrants who escaped from a Communist re-education camp. They made it to the United States with no money and an eighth-grade education. Since no one would hire them, they opened up a Chinese restaurant in Eugene, Oregon. And we lived in a small and poorer neighboring town, Springfield, Oregon, where I was born and raised.

There were six of us in my family, living in a 1400-square-foot house. I started at the age of five working in the restaurant. Even then, I constantly worried about the restaurant going under. It was hard not having stability.

As a kid, I feared becoming homeless, and as a result, I grew up working my tail off. I dreamt of having a future job where I could use my brain instead of physical labor to make money—

one where I would get to wear suits and make a lot of money. I envisioned myself as confident and important—someone that people respected.

After graduating from college, I decided to go into sales as part of a startup with a major company that was dominating the B2C (business to consumer) market but was completely new in the B2B (business to business) market—new products, new offerings, new everything.

I started two weeks after the rest of the team since I was finishing up my senior year in college. So I was nervous even before my first day, knowing everyone else had a head start on me. I had the additional pressure of having to prove to my parents that I was doing the right thing. They wanted me to be something more prestigious such as a doctor, a lawyer, or an accountant.

What made them even more upset was that I had interviewed and received five job offers with starting salaries up to around $60K and this B2B opportunity was the lowest paying of all of them at $29,500. So here I was, turning down all these other higher-paying opportunities to take a chance on this company that I saw as a growth opportunity. I wanted to prove my parents wrong and show them that I could make good decisions.

I memorized the product manual and was so pumped for my first day. I was going to work hard and be the best! They introduced me to my boss, who had never done this job before, and handed me a sales manual written in the 1980s. It was a bunch of garbage, so I asked my boss what I should do.

My boss told me that sales is a numbers game. He said, "Marcus, I want you to book some meetings. Go outside, start walking into businesses, and book some appointments."

I said, "Ok, where should I go?"

He replied, "Open the door, walk outside, and go right."

I didn't even have any business cards yet, so he gave me a stack of his that were stapled into a bunch of brochures.

I said, "I like to have metrics. How many offices should I go into?"

"If you can get into 30, you should be able to book one or two appointments today."

I thought it would be relatively easy. After growing up working in the restaurant business, I never met a stranger, and I was not a stranger to hard work. That first day I walked into over 60 businesses ... and I didn't book a single appointment.

I remember sitting in my car at the end of that day with 60 business cards scattered all around me, no meetings booked, no interest generated.

The next day, I hit the pavement again and went to 60 completely different businesses. Same result: no interest, no booked meetings.

I was in disbelief because if what my boss said was true, sheer numbers say I should have generated some interest. How can sales be so hard? I had no idea what I was doing wrong.

I went to my boss the next day and asked him what I should do. "Call them," he said.

"What?"

"Call all the people on the business cards that you collected."

I got on the phone and I went through all 120 cards ... and I still didn't book a single meeting.

I was starting to freak out at this point. How could I have 240 touches between door knocks and phone calls with ZERO booked meetings? It didn't make any sense.

I went back to my boss and asked him again what I should do. "Hey Marcus, like I told you, it's a numbers game. The more hands you shake, the more money you make. You just have to work harder. Call them again."

So I went back to my desk and called them all again. At this point, I had made 240 phone calls and walked into over 120 businesses—and no meetings. I was now wondering what I had gotten myself into. Why didn't I take one of those other jobs?!

My parents told me they were right and I was wrong. They just knew I had made a huge mistake. I started second-guessing myself. *Maybe I can't do this,* I thought. *What if I can't make this work and I lose my job and have to move back home?*

And what was even worse was that I saw peers on my team who were booking meetings. Not any huge numbers, but they were doing more than I was, and I didn't think that they were working very hard. I for sure had outworked everyone that first week with nothing to show for it.

I remember that night complaining about it all to my girlfriend (who is now my wife).

"The economy is bad, and I have the worst territory."

"I have an awful boss who doesn't have a clue about selling, and he isn't coaching me or helping me."

"I've made a terrible mistake."

It was a total pity party.

So my girlfriend looks at me and says, "What are you going to do? Why don't you get some books on selling?"

So I went to the public library that weekend and I checked out about 10 books by authors like Zig Ziglar and Brian Tracy, all the classic sales books. I started reading them voraciously.

I outworked all my peers, but six weeks later, they were closing deals, and I had yet to close even one! They were not working a fraction of the time I was, and on top of that, they were making fun of me.

I was in panic mode because I was the worst rep in the division. Even worse, I felt super slimy and salesy with the approach we were supposed to use. They just kept telling me to badger more people—make more calls, send more emails, work harder.

The worst part was what started going on in my head. The mental anguish, the anxiety, and the fear. When you don't live up to your own expectations, it destroys you mentally. I was seeing zero progress and wondering why I was banging my head against the wall.

On Sunday nights I would be scared and nervous. I couldn't focus because I knew that Monday would bring more rejection, more people telling me no, more people chewing me out. I had people pulling guns on me, I had dogs biting me on in-person cold calls, and I was freaking out.

I wasn't making any money, I was worried about paying rent and getting groceries, and the economy was falling apart. I wanted to propose to my girlfriend, but I didn't have any money. I needed to prove myself to her parents as well as my own.

On top of that, my boss had even threatened me that he would have to fire me if I didn't make some sales. I was struggling. I had zero confidence and was stressed out of my mind.

I had three options:

- Figure it out.

- Get fired trying.

- Quit and try to get another sales job in a totally unrelated sales field.

This all happened during the last recession, and the job market was not great, so I didn't like options two or three. I know this sounds cliché, but this was when I found Tony Robbins' book *Awaken the Giant Within*, which was one of my first turning points. He says that if you don't like the answer, ask a better question. I realized that I had been asking myself a lot of bad questions.

Once I realized this, I started asking myself better questions. For instance, if I had a bad cold call, and they hung up on me or cussed me out for calling them, I started shifting my thinking to ask different questions: "What can I learn from this? What can I do differently? How can I shift my tonality to get a better-desired result?" I went from a problem-focused way of thinking to a solution-based way of thinking. I tested different approaches and eventually started having better results.

After a few more weeks of pure struggle, I discovered the exact secrets outlined in this book that accelerated my results and skyrocketed me to #1 during my third month of sales. Instead of just pitching, I started asking better questions on sales calls. They would tell me what they wanted, and I would sell them what they needed. It was actually very simple, and the amazing part is that I didn't feel sleazy doing it.

I held the #1 spot for the next three months, and then I was asked to be a peer leader over the worst operational team in my division. Despite having a brand-new unworked territory with zero pipeline and more responsibility, I was fortunate to stay #1 in that company for the next six months, earning two more promotions and winning more awards.

I was then fortunate enough to achieve some of these cool things:

- Generated over $700M in sales over the last decade

- Promoted 10X in 10 years at two Fortune 500 companies

- Hit and exceeded quota up to 250% for 13 consecutive years

- Won countless awards such as President's Club

- Helped over 50+ employees to earn President's Club

- Trained thousands of others to achieve massive sales success

Every year I sold more, earning close to seven figures annually, including equity. I continually exceeded my quota and kept getting promoted. In my last role, I was leading a sales organization of 110+ employees.

I learned a long time ago, way before I ever started leading teams of people, that in sales or anything else you do in life, if you just work hard enough, you'll make a living and you'll be fine.

But one day, I remember having a major epiphany after reading a quote I found by Jim Rohn which said, "If you work hard at your job, you make a living. If you work hard on yourself, you'll make a fortune."

I found this to be wildly true. When I started working hard on myself, I became better with prospects. I became better in relationships. I became better with money. I became better across the board.

Once I understood this principle, I applied it in my work life with my team. When I started hiring salespeople and leading teams, I did the same thing: helped them become the best version of themselves. The quota numbers took care of themselves.

Over the years, as I brought in new hires, I would work with them to uncover ALL their goals. Not just finding out their extrinsic motivation but also uncovering their intrinsic motivators to discover what was really driving them.

A salesperson would say, "Marcus, I want to earn $200K this year."

My response would take it to the next level. "That's great.

What is the significance for you of $200K?"

"Well, it's more money than I'm making now."

"Ok, great. What do you want to do with it?"

"I want to invest more."

"What would you like to invest in?"

"Well, maybe real estate or my 401K."

"Why do you want to do that?"

"Well, I don't want to worry about money. I grew up very poor and we lived paycheck to paycheck. We ate ramen every day or beans and rice. It was really tough and it broke up my parent's marriage."

I use this method to peel back the layers to reveal their intrinsic motivators so I can help them to achieve their goals. It isn't about helping them make $200K. It's about helping them to build a bulletproof mindset and confidence so that they can have the stability that they desire.

If I can give them the tools to accomplish that, I'm going to help them do it. So what would happen is that they would hit their goals, and that would help me to hit my goals as a team leader. They would stay longer and we would develop a deeper bond than just a manager/employee relationship. I became a mentor who helped them reach their goals in *every* area of their lives.

With my employees, I used to jokingly say, "You might hate me for 30 days for challenging and pushing you, but you're going to love me on day 31 because of who you become, the money you will make, and the life you are going to create."

I now use these same principles and techniques in my own business, coaching others on how to be the best version of themselves. They find that when everything flows, the money comes. The output is the result of the input. The fruits are determined by the roots. So if you work on the roots, the fruits will come.

As a leader, I use the same techniques I learned in the Sales CODE Selling System: you **C**onnect, you **O**pen, you **D**irect, and you **E**xpand. If I do it at a deep level, I can help people tap into their inner potential and achieve things that they never thought possible.

Most people only scratch the tip of the iceberg. They get scared and need someone to tell them it's possible and to show them the way to get there. If you have someone to help guide, push, inspire, and challenge you, whether you like it or not, then you'll become the best version of yourself, which will ultimately lead to achieving the fortune and freedom you want.

Who This Book Is For

When Kim came in to interview with me, she had very little sales experience. As an entry-level salesperson for a mom-and-pop insurance company, she lacked real sales training.

But I could see a hunger in her and a drive to be successful. Even though she didn't have a successful track record, I went with my gut and hired her to my new team.

It was hard for her in the beginning. She had to learn how to prospect: how to cold call, how to run a sales call … It was all new to her. I taught her how to have conversion conversations. We went over sales psychology and how to adjust her style to fit her prospects. I explained how to get them to open up and have a real conversation.

Fast forward a year and a half, and Kim became the number 1 rep in the company! She hit President's Club, broke quite a few records, and was promoted.

She became a whole new person. Her transformation transcended across the board, from the level of confidence she exudes to how she communicates. Now she can accurately read rooms, adjust her style to build trust, and quickly gain likeability.

Like Kim, you don't need to be a "born" salesperson. Whether you are brand new, have 20+ years of sales experience, or are somewhere in between, you just need the drive to succeed, the desire to improve, some simple frameworks, and a mentor or guide. If you'll bring the first half (drive and desire), this book will provide the second half (frameworks and guide).

Scripts Vs. Frameworks

Great actors and actresses have a script, but *how* they deliver their lines determines the impact. Everything matters—tonality, inflection, pace, pauses—even their personalities. Once they know their lines well, they can then adjust on the fly based on how their partner in the scene acts and reacts. While there are specific lines for them to memorize, those lines act as a *framework* for the scene.

This book is designed to be your "skeleton" framework. Yes, there will be scripts for you to learn, but your delivery of those scripts will make them come to life, kind of like how muscles move the bones of a skeleton. A skeleton can't move without the muscle, and the muscle needs the skeleton's form. You need *both* to make the body work.

Striving to be a top salesperson is much the same. Whether you are new to the field or a seasoned rep who wants to achieve the next level, make more money, and change the trajectory of your life, within the pages of this book, you will find valuable tools, frameworks, downloadable worksheets, and insights to achieve your goals.

SECTION TWO

FILLING YOUR FUNNEL

When you can master sales at the highest level, you'll never worry about money ever again.

A Full Pipeline Is Your Lifeline

When I first got started in sales, there was a guy on my team named Tim. Tim was a phenomenal closer. He was great at getting the deal, but he relied 100% on inbound leads to get his prospects.

Once I figured out how to sell and generate my own prospects, I could run circles around Tim. The economy started getting tough, so his inbound leads dwindled while I generated my own leads through outbound methods. My ability to prospect was a real game changer.

Here's what I learned: Being a great closer will only get you so far. If you are not able to get in front of enough qualified prospects, it's hard to be consistently successful.

Being a pro at outbound prospecting means that your pipeline will always be full, and you won't have to rely on marketing or other people to fill up your calendar with leads. It boosts your confidence knowing you have plenty of opportunities to close. And it helps eliminate the "commission breath" some get when they realize they have a scarce pipeline close to quarter end.

So how do you prospect like a pro? Well, it starts with knowing who your customer is, where they are, and what they want.

Once you know these things, you can master what I learned early on that completely changed my entire trajectory.

It's called the "Whisper Test."

Mastering the Whisper Test

Imagine this: Your prospect is at dinner with their spouse and you come over to them, a complete stranger, and you whisper in their ear, "Hey, I know you are struggling with [fill in the blank X], and [Y] makes you so stressed and makes you want to quit and [Z] is giving you the most stress. I can get rid of all that for you. Would you like to hear?"

These people who don't even know who you are want to rush away from the dinner table to sit and talk with you because they have no idea how you know so much about them at such a deep level. You know about their deepest fears, stresses, and desires as if you can read their mind and hear their thoughts. They need to talk to you now and know more about you. That's the Whisper Test.

Once you know enough about your prospect to put them through the Whisper Test, you can achieve the ranks of all of the top performers. You have the power to determine your own success.

7 Simple Tips for Fast Results

The following seven super simple tips, which you can implement immediately, will put you far ahead of your competition.

When you understand the importance of consistently prospecting—and you do it well—you will soar beyond your most ambitious goals.

The biggest difference I see between top performers and low performers is that top performers master these tips and low performers skip them. And then the low performers struggle to understand why others are getting results while they're staying stuck.

These seven tips are at the front of this book for a reason. I am not going to make you dig for them. I want you to read them, start practicing them, and come back and read them again. Write them down. Review them multiple times. Make them as natural as brushing your teeth or driving a car.

These tips work effectively in a down economy and AMAZING in an up economy. No experience or tech is required—you simply need to execute and you will get results!

Tip #1: Get Crystal Clear on Your Ideal Customer (Because the Riches Are in the Niches)

Have you ever had your sales manager say to you, "It's a numbers game"? Or, "Smile and dial"? What about, "The more hands you shake, the more money you make"?

Mine did, and these sayings could not be further from the truth.

Remember how many hands I shook early on in my career, to no avail? You have to become CRYSTAL CLEAR on who your ideal customer is *before* you start prospecting.

On my first day in outside sales, my boss told me to do the spray and pray method—go after anyone and everyone. He told me to knock on as many doors as I could.

As I mentioned earlier, I took off and went knocking on doors and then made hundreds of phone calls with ZERO booked appointments, let alone any sales. What I didn't mention was that I eventually called up a rep from our company in another state that was having pretty solid success despite the recession. I asked her how she was getting appointments. She shared with me her very simple strategy.

She called on prospects that she had seen with fleets of box trucks, which made a lot of sense as we leased and rented box trucks. Her logic was that if they had trucks, they had a need or would eventually have a need for more trucks.

It clicked. I had been calling on businesses in totally different markets and industries. I was trying so hard to *convince* prospects who would have ZERO need for my product.

It was like trying to sell steaks to a vegan!

My product was not for the mass market but that had been my approach to prospecting. We were not diverse like Amazon, which has something for everyone. We were more like a boutique shop, which meant distinct customers, a distinct approach, and distinct messaging.

That night, I started making a list of key characteristics of ideal customers. I hyper-focused on niche industries that had the highest likelihood of using my company.

After about 15 minutes, I had a pretty good list. (Shocker—not a single one that I had called in the past week was remotely close to being an ideal customer!)

The next day, I did a search for companies that matched my new parameters.

I started dialing. After four hours, I had booked four appointments! It wasn't anything crazy, but that was four more appointments than I had ever booked, so I was ecstatic!

But here's what's even more fascinating—the more targeted the niche list, the better the calls. It meant that I made fewer calls and booked more appointments.

Fast-forward three months, as I continued to refine my sales process and scripts, I shot up to #1, and I held the #1 spot for the next three months.

Three months later, I was asked to take over a completely different territory, causing me to lose my pipeline and start over with zero customers.

I took what I had learned, and I went into this new territory hyper-focused on the right target market. As the saying goes: "The riches are in the niches."

As you map out your target market, or ICP (ideal customer profile), you want to think about:

- What industry is your target market in?

- What are some key characteristics that make them ideal?

- Who are the typical decision-makers?

- What is most important for them?

- What is your value proposition for them?

- How can you contact them?

- What are their desires and pain points?

As you are refining your niche, here are some questions you might have:

Q: What if I don't know what niche to go after?

Keep it simple. Do you have existing clients and customers? If so, what industries are they in? Start with those and expand out based on similar functions.

Q: What if I don't have enough leads or opportunities in this specific niche?

Remember, even if you are super niched down, once you maximize the opportunity in that niche, span out based on similar functions. Don't focus on not having enough leads.

When I started out, I was given the smallest territory. Everyone else had eight zip codes, but I only had four. I had to open my eyes and shift my thinking to bring about success. Get creative!

Q: I sell to everyone. Shouldn't I target everyone?

When you niche down, you can better connect with the prospects. You can target niche by niche to maximize your conversion.

For example, let's say you sell a payroll software. Technically, you can sell those to everyone who has a business. But if you want to sell to Bill who owns a bar and grill versus a CTO (chief technology officer) at a mid-size tech company, you have to have very different messaging.

To summarize, niching down results in faster and better results.

Tip #2: Quality Lists Lead to Quality Results

Most companies have some sort of CRM (customer relationship management) system with purchased data or lists. Unfortunately, most mediocre sales managers will tell you to just "dial down the list."

This may seem fine until you realize that data changes *all the time*. What was accurate one week ago may not be accurate today. So prepare for call block sessions by doing the research before you dial!

Let me share with you an example. In 2011, I started with a brand new company. On day one, I was given a printed list to dial off of. After the first 20 or so dials, I immediately found there were many disconnected numbers and incorrect names.

I pushed through the first day on the phone and booked seven appointments. However, I felt *exhausted*. There was so much cleanup of data, and I had to go through 80+ dials to get those few meetings.

I knew this was a simple solve, so I asked my manager to give me the list in advance or let me build my own.

I took half of the next day and just did research. I looked up business types, decision-maker info, social media, news articles, etc.

The result?

I booked seven appointments in half the time. Before I called, I made sure I had the right names of the decision-makers and some basic info. This ensured that I wasn't going to call a disconnected number and that my phone conversations would be more productive.

And if you're an AE (account executive) who has an SDR/BDR (sales or business development rep) booking for you, I'll tell you right now, the AEs that consistently crush it *also* consistently book their own meetings as well.

If you are making calls off a general list without names or other pertinent info, you are doing yourself a disservice by not taking the time to properly prepare and do the necessary research.

There are so many resources available to get the decision-maker's name, and if you can't find it, you can use my Seeker Script in Tip #3 to call the company and get the info you need.

First, build your target market list by niching down and being very specific. This will give you more quality dials, and when you have more quality dials, you'll be more motivated to keep dialing!

Next, search online for the decision-maker's name. If you can't find it, then set time aside to call those prospects with only the goal of updating your records.

You'd be shocked at the responses you get when you simply focus on collecting information with zero pressure of booking meetings. Then, during your next call block, you can run through the list of quality dials and focus on booking qualified meetings.

This one SIMPLE approach improved my results by 75% AND required less time on the phone. As the saying goes, "Those who fail to prepare are preparing to fail!"

The key is consistency.

I would block a few hours every Friday afternoon to do a little bit of research. It gave me an edge and helped me achieve results faster than anyone else.

Build time in to research beforehand and you'll see your results skyrocket on the phones.

Tip #3: How to Fly Through Gatekeepers

Gatekeepers can be tough to get through! And here's the reality: if you are not able to get past the gatekeeper, then nothing matters.

The best ones protect the decision-maker like no other and block you out. Early on, I learned the BEST way to get through gatekeepers is to use a simple ethical persuasion principle that has been around for thousands of years.

I used to get shut down by gatekeepers. They would send me to voicemail, give me an excuse like "They're in a meeting," or find some creative way to get me off the phone. That is, until I made a very important discovery.

Here's what I learned ...

One day I was sitting in the lobby about 15 minutes early for my next appointment. I sat within eight feet of the receptionist who was receiving call after call after call.

In those 15 minutes, she answered 10+ calls, and I could hear each one! (Yes, I casually eavesdropped.) There were salespeople who called that sounded just like me. Friendly, outgoing, chipper, with a short pitch. Once she heard their friendly voice, I could see her get annoyed as she directed them straight to voicemail.

Then I observed two different calls. Both calls she immediately directed to the right department heads. I noticed that both callers did NOT even say who they were with and their tone was very direct.

Once the gatekeeper heard their tone, she immediately transferred without hesitation.

It clicked. Those direct callers *did not* sound like a typical salesperson. They sounded like authority figures.

Picture someone of authority. This could be a judge, a police officer, a prestigious doctor, or a CRO (chief revenue officer) of a large organization. How do they speak? That's how these direct callers sounded.

They *commanded* the conversation with the words they used, their tone, pace, inflection, and their presence. They spoke as if they already knew the person they were calling, and that got them through.

So the question was this: If the gatekeeper believed that I was an authority figure, a.k.a. a person of power, and that the decision-maker knew me, would she send me to them with fewer or zero objections?

I decided to test my hypothesis the next day. On every single call I made, I was direct, firm, and did not pitch.

I acted as if they already knew me. I acted as if I was an authority figure.

I felt super uncomfortable, but the results? I was able to speak with *every* single decision-maker that was there, and I booked most of them!

This completely changed the game for me, and I've done it this way ever since.

I learned later on that I was leveraging the Law of Authority, a principle that has been around for thousands of years and was also made popular in Robert Cialdini's book, *Influence*. In a nutshell, it says that one of the most powerful ways to become a person of influence is to establish your authority and credibility through how you speak and carry yourself.

The moral of the story:

Don't act like a salesperson when speaking to the gatekeeper.

A good gatekeeper can tell the difference between a customer and a salesperson, a prospective lead and a vendor—by nothing more than the tone of their voice. If the gatekeeper suspects you are a salesperson, it's going to be tough to get through.

Speaking with authority and knowing the decision-maker's name (remember: do your research!) is super important. Being direct and firm and sounding more like a customer or a prospective lead always converts at a higher level.

BONUS TIP

If you're wondering what to say, I've got you covered. Following are two specific scripts you can use. This first script is the Pit Bull Script to get past the gatekeeper. It's a pattern interrupt and it's highly effective. I've tested this technique across the country and even internationally. The second is the Seeker Script. It's much softer and can be used when you can't find the name of the gatekeeper in your research.

Pit Bull Script

For this script, you want to be direct, firm, and have short answers. Less is more here.

This script is going to make most salespeople uncomfortable, but it is incredibly effective.

The first step: Know the name of the decision-maker you are trying to reach. I will discuss how to get that information later.

Here is a sample call:

Salesperson: *May I speak with John? Thanks.*

Say this in a firm, confident voice. Ending with thanks creates a statement, not a question. You are not being angry or rude, just firm.

Gatekeeper: *Who can I say is calling?*

Salesperson: *It's Marcus. Thanks.*

I'm not saying "My name is Marcus," or "This is Marcus." I'm assuming they know who I am, and when I say thanks, I'm ending the conversation.

Don't give any further information, including the company you work for. Keep it short and direct. This forces the gatekeeper to ask more questions. The reality is that at this point they are unsure about who you are. Are you an angry customer, a vendor, or a personal friend? If you do this verbatim, you will see that you can bypass a majority of gatekeepers at this point.

Now, some will ask you what company you are with which is very normal.

> Gatekeeper: *What company are you with?*

> Salesperson: *Chan's Cybersecurity Services, thanks.*

Again, give them very little information. If they still don't transfer you, they may ask:

> Gatekeeper: *What is this regarding?*

> Salesperson: *In reference to a cybersecurity program I set up with XYZ Company.*

Because you are giving such little bits of information, it forces the gatekeeper to keep asking questions, which will make them uncomfortable. They will want to transfer you because they are afraid they might mess up an important call. What you want to avoid is getting into a conversation with the gatekeeper.

Now, I know there will be some of you who read this and think, *Well, I don't think this is going to work for me.* But I'm telling you right now, this is a highly effective and very powerful script. It just takes practice, so give it a try, and remember that attitude and tonality are everything.

Seeker Script

This script is very different from the Pit Bull Script. It's especially useful if you don't know who the decision-maker is, if you aren't sure the data you have is correct, or if you can't find anything online.

In this script, your tone is much softer, and it is going to be very inquisitive. Don't sound like you are trying to sell. Your primary goal is to gather information—get the decision-maker's name and any other information they may offer to you. If they transfer you, even better!

> Salesperson: *Hi, this is a sales call. Do you want to hang up?*

This usually throws them off. They may laugh it off or say something like, "Well, that depends, what's this all about?"

> Salesperson: *My name is Marcus with Chan's Cyber-security Services. I'm actually hoping that you can help me out. It's my job to update our records. We help businesses with their cybersecurity protocols, so who's in charge of making decisions regarding that?*

You asked an open-ended question. You have told them you are just doing your job, and they can connect with that.

At this point, they will either give you the name or tell you they already have someone taking care of that. If the latter is the response you get, then respond with something like this:

> Salesperson: *I totally get that. I'm just doing my job and hoping you can help me out.*

Laugh, be friendly, and adjust this to your style to try and get whatever info you can. Once you get that name, you can call back the next day and use the Pit Bull Script.

Starting with the seeker gatekeeper script is a great hack if you are new to your role and don't have any information or you have a list of bad names.

Here's a second hack: if you are calling into a mid-size or larger business, they will usually have a sales department. Ask for that department and you will probably get a salesperson on the line. You can run through the same script, but the cool part is that most salespeople will want to be friendly and help you.

Tip #4: Track Your Critical Core Ratios

Bad sales managers tell you to "play the numbers game" by "making more calls" or "sending more emails."

Now, it is true that you could just double the number of outbound calls and emails, and theoretically, you might double your results. But who wants to work twice as many hours as needed?

The truth is that top reps play the "numbers game" the *right* way and know what numbers/ratios to actually measure.

Start by understanding which key metrics are important for whichever outbound medium has you focusing your efforts—calls, emails, or LinkedIn messages. Then, make the *right* adjustments based on *facts*.

Let's use outbound calling as an example.

Although there are tons of metrics you can definitely track, for the sake of simplicity, here are the ones we'll focus on:

Weekly number of dials. This is the total number of cold, initial outbound calls you dial in a week.

Gatekeeper bypass ratio. This is the percentage of dials that get sent to the decision-maker.

Ex: You speak to 20 gatekeepers and you get sent to the decision-maker 1 time.

1/20 = 5% gatekeeper bypass ratio

Number of decision-makers spoken to. This is the average number of decision-makers you actually speak to, and in turn, have a chance to book.

Number of appointments booked off decision-makers. This is how many you booked.

Appointment booking ratio. This is how many appointments you booked divided by the total number of decision-makers you spoke to.

Ex: You spoke to 10 decision-makers and you booked 4.

4/10 = 40% appointment booking ratio

Out of these metrics, the two most important ratios that increase your booking efficiency are your gatekeeper bypass ratio and your appointment booking ratio.

Meaning, the *higher* your gatekeeper bypass ratio and appointment booking ratio, the more efficient you are. If your ratios are low, it's signaling the exact areas you must improve to get better results.

Because they are ratios, you can apply these same principles whether you are selling to the SMB (small to midsize businesses) or to the Enterprise space (big businesses that may be publicly traded).

Let's use a simple example with the gatekeeper bypass and appointment booking ratios:

Weekly number of dials: Let's say you make on average 125 outbound dials/week.

Gatekeeper bypass ratio: Let's say out of 125 dials, 10 get sent to the decision-maker.

Gatekeeper bypass ratio = 10/125 = 8%

Number of decision-makers spoken to: For simplicity's sake, let's say 10 answer the phone.

Number of appointments booked off decision-makers: You book 5 appointments out of the 10 that you speak with.

Appointment booking ratio = 5/10 = 50%

GATEKEEPER BYPASS RATIO

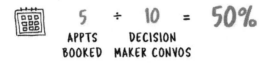

10 ÷ 125 = 8%
DECISION   DIALS
MAKER CONVOS

APPOINTMENT BOOKING RATIO

5 ÷ 10 = 50%
APPTS   DECISION
BOOKED   MAKER CONVOS

Now, the average manager will tell a rep that to go from 5 to 10 appointments, they simply need to increase from 125 dials to 250 dials. It makes logical sense only if you want to double your working hours. (You don't.)

Top reps want to work smarter, not more hours, so they now start "hacking" their sales process, leveraging the two ratios.

Let's start in reverse with the numbers we've discussed so far...

Appointment Booking Ratio

If you're booking 5 out of 10 appointments, making your appointment booking ratio 50%, how can you improve the way you run that initial call?

Can you improve:

- What you say?

- What you ask?

- Your tonality?

- Your pace?

- Your inflection?

- How you overcome objections?

When you start thinking this way and start making the right changes, that 50% could easily shift to 60–90%, meaning you are now booking 6–9 appointments *without* making more calls. (For the majority of industries, if your appointment booking ratio is less than 70–80%, chances are very high you need to improve this ratio).

Gatekeeper Bypass Ratio

If you're averaging 10 calls getting sent to the decision-maker (number of decision-makers spoken to) out of every 125 calls you make (8% gatekeeper bypass ratio), how can you improve this number?

Can you improve:

- Your targeting? (The ICP, role, industry, account size, etc.)

- What you say?

- How you say it?

- Timing?

- Prep?

- The data you have?

- The time you call?

- The days you call?

What if you could improve it from 8% to 12–13%? That leads to 15–16 decision-makers you get to speak with. Even with a 50% appointment booking ratio, now you're at 7–8 appointments booked.

If you improve your appointment booking ratio to 60–90% in addition to that, now you're booking 9–14 appointments. (If your current GBR is <10%, chances are quite high you need to improve this too.)

Work Smarter, Not Harder

You can see that these two core ratios are powerful when it comes to improving your results. When you get clarity on these ratios and start working to improve them, you'll find out what it means to "work smarter, not harder."

Talk to top reps across the board, and you'll discover that they actually make significantly fewer calls (cold outbound) than everyone else, yet they close *more* than everyone else.

Tip #5: Crafting Conversion Conversations

Have you ever answered a phone call from a telemarketer?

Once you answer, they go into a 60-second pitch about what a great product they have. Most of them are given a lengthy sales pitch to begin with and then they are told it's a numbers game.

So every day they play the high rejection game, trying to get through the gatekeepers, low response to emails, and low connect rates to decision-makers. They just assume that's how it's "supposed to be done."

I was a brand new sales manager, benchmarking with a team in San Jose, California. I was in the bullpen with two other reps, Jorge and Carlos. Both were new but pretty decent reps. Still, I could see them struggling on the phones.

I asked them if they were open to some coaching because at this point they had been calling for a while and hadn't made a single appointment.

They agreed, so I started diving deep into their challenges, and they shared how frustrating and demoralizing it was to keep having gatekeepers shut them down. And if they were able to get through, the decision-maker always seemed to be "in a meeting" or busy.

They felt frustrated that when they did get hold of a decision-maker, they would *still* get shut down. I knew that by the law of averages (which states that if you do something long enough, a ratio will begin to appear), they would eventually book some appointments and even close some deals, but they would hate their job in the process. They already felt like quitting.

I told them not to quit! The issue they had was that they were speaking a different language than their prospects.

I explained that the words and questions they were using were not the same as the niche industry they were speaking to. In essence, it's as if their prospects were speaking Chinese and they were talking to them in English.

There is a disconnect between the messaging and the audience which automatically leads to fewer meetings and deals. This applies across the board to cold calls, emails, copy, and physical letters.

They were still kind of confused, so I talked to them about the perfect prospect avatar. The mistake many people make is that they aren't thinking about their target market's psychographics (hopes, fears, attitudes, and values). They are focusing on a specific industry, job function, title, and maybe some basic demographics (age and income, for instance).

Although those can help, you have to niche down even more. The prospect must feel as if you are reading their mind.

Psychographics go way deeper than basic demographics and include the following:

- What are their deepest desires?

- What are their deepest needs and wants?

- What are their deepest fears?

- What makes them worry?

- What are their biggest hot buttons?

- What drives them crazy?

- What frustrates them more than anything else?

- What are their biggest internal limiting beliefs?

- What are their biggest external limiting beliefs?

- What would remove their stress?

What's even more important to know is the "why" behind each one. This is going into the psyche of the prospect. They should feel as if you are in their head. It should pass the whisper test.

All of your messaging must be customized as a framework—a conversion conversation—to fit the perfect prospect avatar.

Jorge, Carlos, and I wrote all this out on a whiteboard. We took the corporate laminated phone script and completely rewrote it into a simple, shorter framework that had the perfect prospect avatar components built-in.

We cut the scripting down from over 60 seconds to about 20–25 seconds. We built out a hyper-targeted niche list of prospects, just like in step one. I could tell they were still kind of on the fence about all of this. I smiled and said, "Trust me."

They started dialing. Within two to three hours, they had each booked eight appointments! They were fired up! It had been taking them at least a week or more to book that many.

They also said the decision-makers were more open to talking with them, and that the conversations were deeper and better than before.

I explained why. Now, decision-makers knew they were talking to someone who was worth their time because they actually feel heard. It was clear it wasn't some poorly-trained rep calling them out of the blue who knew nothing about their business.

They came off as an expert to their prospects. This is so important. You want your prospects to believe that *you* are the expert.

As a result of crafting simple, hyper-personalized conversion conversations, their booking ratio skyrocketed, and they booked more quality leads than ever before.

This applies to all types of messaging, including emails, direct messaging, and video messaging.

I became very good friends with these guys. Both of their incomes continued to skyrocket, they hit President's Club every year, and they got promoted multiple times, creating a better life for their families.

The cool part is anyone can do this.

How do you learn the inner depths of what's on your perfect prospect's mind?

It's easier than you might think. Go where they hang out. Find forums, chat rooms, and community groups. If you pay really close attention to the conversations, you will see questions and comments that will tell you exactly what you want to know.

Heck, check out the reviews on third-party review sites for your competitors or your company. They will share everything you want to know and exactly what they like, hate, and more.

You might be thinking, *That sounds like it will take some time.* And you're right. It will take some time. But picture it as a one-time, upfront investment that will pay you dividends for the rest of your life.

So what's next? How do you write out the messaging for cold calls, emails, and direct messages?

Here's the key: keep it super simple and as short as possible. Remember that you are interrupting the prospect when you call. Their mind is focused on whatever task they were doing, and your call interrupts them. Complexity creates friction in mental processing, so the easier it is to understand your message, the higher it will convert.

Imagine that each word you write and will eventually say is going to cost you $100. Keep your cost as low as possible without sacrificing the quality of the message. Then test and refine until you get the booking ratio and the response ratio that you desire.

In a nutshell, if you'll create hyper-personalized conversion conversation frameworks, you'll book more and close more. The key is to simplify to multiply your results.

Tip #6: Constructing a Customer-Centric Sales System

In my first two months of attempting sales calls, I was at the very bottom of the sales team ranking. I was struggling. Around this time, my boss pulled me into his office at 4 p.m. on a Friday, and he threatened me with a PIP (performance improvement plan). I was more scared and lost than ever as I had no idea what to do to improve my results.

The following week I had my yearly physical. It was pretty normal except for my blood pressure, which had increased pretty significantly since the prior year. I wasn't all that surprised as I was super stressed.

My doctor recommended some changes in my diet and exercise. It was pretty much the opposite of what I had been doing. I was used to eating tons of carbs like pizza, pasta, and rice, and only lifting weights. I was a former competitive swimmer, so I was used to eating a lot every day, but I was eating like I was still competing and still in college. She told me to eat more fruits and veggies, cut out sugar and salt, and do cardio three to five times a week, along with the weight training.

I was actually very excited to make all these changes. I thought to myself, *How did my doctor convince me to completely change my behavior with my eating and workout habits? How did she "sell" me or persuade me to be willingly open to changing behaviors that I had been doing for over a decade?*

Here's the thing. She didn't sell me at all. She barely talked. I talked the entire time. As I thought more about the visit, I realized that she kept asking me more and more questions.

I realized she knew my goal was to get healthy, so she asked me questions to cover all my problems, needs, and desires. Then she aligned a simple solution for all my problems, needs, and desires. And the thing was, even before she made a recommendation, I was already sold on making a change based on the 15 minutes of questions she asked.

She knew the goal and worked backward to get there. As a patient, I felt really good about it.

A lightbulb went off! I could apply the same concept to a sales process. I could reverse the sales process, begin with my prospect's end goals in mind, and then ask questions to figure out *their* problems, needs, and desires. Then I could align my solution with what I uncovered.

This made sense to me because I had been doing the opposite. I had started out barely asking any questions and trying to pitch 90% of the time. I was going to the appointments, asking a few questions, and then dropping as many features and benefits about our product as possible. I could see on their faces that they didn't like that, and they couldn't wait for me to leave. It was not a customer-centric process.

So that night, I sat down and began with their end goals in mind. I mapped out the questions I would need to ask to get there. It was like going on a road trip. I knew the end destination, so I mapped out backward the questions I would have to ask to get there.

I tested it the next day. I went to my appointments and spent 90% of the time asking questions and only 10% actually presenting, aligning the presentation based on what I learned from the answers to the questions.

I only had five appointments that day, but I closed four of them. They were small deals, but I closed 80% with this method. My results accelerated *immediately*. That's when I knew I was onto something.

This is a customer-centric system. It was not about my company, my solution, or me. It was all focused on the customer in the same way my doctor had focused on me, the patient.

Then I had a bigger realization: it wasn't just the discovery part of the sales process where I asked questions, but it all started with the mindset.

Asking the right internal questions reframed my mind and impacted every single part of my sales process—everything from prospecting to discovery to presenting the demo to closing to handling objections to account growth and even customer success.

This is how true experts really sell. The more trust and credibility they create through powerful, insightful questions, the more they position themselves as the expert.

This ultimately leads to more meetings, more closed deals, more commissions, and simply just feeling great about how they sell, as they are truly serving the customer.

Now, in two to three hours, I was booking 8–10 new appointments. I finished out the month at #1, having 5X the results of the second-place rep. I held that spot for nine months in a row while earning two more promotions. All of this was due to executing a refined customer-centric sales system and process.

When you focus on the customer and ask more of the right questions for every single part of the sales process, your results will go up. The better you get at this, the more appointments you will book, the more deals you will close, the more you will exceed your quota, and the more you will earn.

I can't overstate this: It's not about making more calls. If you focus on refining every part of your sales process and asking better questions, you will be able to get better results with the same amount of effort.

At this point, you may be trying to figure out which questions to ask.

If you have done the past few steps, you have already done some of the heavy lifting. Now is the time to start working backward and figure out the questions that lead to the answer you are looking for.

Don't I need experience to know what to ask?

You don't. You do need to do some research, and as you gain experience, you can refine the questions further. It's all about imperfect action. You will get a result and then you can refine it from there.

Won't it seem like I'm interrogating them?

Just like anything else, you want to make it conversational. Keep an eye on your tone and how you ask the questions.

Don't I need to spend a lot of time trying to pitch them?

You actually do not. One of the biggest mistakes sales professionals make is going into information overload on their prospects—they share every possible feature and benefit, even if the prospect has not shared their specific issue that the feature would solve. Informational overload leaves the prospect feeling overwhelmed, and then they need more time to process what you have told them.

Keep it simple, and only present on what you uncover in the discovery.

Tip #7: Getting Your External and Internal Environments Organized

This may not seem like it should be under tips for fast sales results, but as I will talk about in Section 9, your mindset and your routine are key components in being successful. Getting your mind into an optimum headspace, as well as being organized, will give you the foundation you need to delve into the next sections of this book.

Desk Prep

Organization is key, especially in your work environment. Whether you have a home office, a work desk, or a cubicle office, make sure it is set up for success.

Think about a professional athlete. They set up their practice arena—their "office"—in a specific way to maximize high performance.

In the same way, your desk or whatever area you use to make calls and do outreach needs to be set up with this same mindset.

Post your goals! This is a very powerful visual reminder to keep you focused. If you are having a rough morning on the phones, which happens to everyone, having your goals top of mind is a great way to stay focused so you can continue to push forward.

Make sure you have your personalized scripts somewhere visible. This is really important because when you are on the phone, you may blank out and forget what to say, but if you have your script in front of you in big, bold letters, you can stay on track. Remember: Scripts are simply frameworks to help keep you on track.

Post some key clientele or customers as references so you can share them as part of your social proof. Post objection handling scripts as well.

Keep a mirror at your desk so you can look yourself in the eye as you are talking and ensure that you are smiling.

Have your CRM open to a single list with your contact names and info. Having two screens is really beneficial, so you can have your calendar open on one of them for easy access to book appointments. You don't want to fumble around looking for open dates and times when you are on the phone. Fumbling around is distracting and could cause you to lose confidence on the phone. Remember, phone calls are all about confidence!

Your desk needs to be clean and uncluttered. When your space is a mess, it's hard to be productive. How do you truly feel when you have junk, old coffee cups, food and snacks, and post-it notes everywhere? Create a clean and organized environment that promotes success.

Mental Prep

Top-tier athletes in any field always mentally prepare before their big event. The same goes for world-class presenters before a big presentation. They do this because it puts them in the right frame of mind and keeps them calm and focused.

You need to do the same thing as well. You don't want to just roll out of bed and go to your office or walk into your home office and start making calls.

I will talk about my morning routine and the importance of creating yours in Section 9. Warming up mentally is critical to your morning routine, but so is preparing for the specific tasks you will be focusing on.

Here are some ideas to get you mentally prepared:

- If you have a commute, take advantage of this time. This is a great time to go through some affirmations to put yourself in that peak, prime-performing state. For instance, a few I like are:

  - "If it is to be, it is up to me!"

  - "It is my duty and responsibility to serve at my highest level!"

  - "I either WIN or I LEARN!"

Choose ones that serve you and make you feel empowered.

- If you are in a physical office with teammates, role-play your first five dials with them. Open by saying the name of the person you are planning to call and role-play as if they are a tough decision-maker. You will be amazed at how well this warms you up.

- If you are in a remote environment, you can still do this. Set up a time and call someone on your team to do this over the phone.

- If you are a lone wolf, role-play out loud. Go all the way from handling the gatekeeper to handling objections. Saying it out loud is really important so you can hear yourself—both what you're saying and how you're saying it.

One of the things that I attribute to my success early on was using these techniques. I had about a 45-minute commute to work each morning, and I used this time to verbally role-play my toughest calls, expecting the worst.

When I got to the office, my brain had been warmed up and I had mapped the neural pathways for my scripting. When I got on the phone and made that first call, I had already said my framework dozens of times.

Calendar Prep

Make sure that you have properly prepared your calendar. If you find that for one hour of phone prospecting, you book one discovery call and your goal is to secure 10 discovery calls per week, you need to be sure that you have blocked the appropriate amount of phone time.

In this example:

10/1 = 10 hours

So when you look at your calendar, you need to be sure that you have at least 10 hours available to be able to meet your goals. It's simple, but most people don't set themselves up for success and then wonder why they are missing their goals.

Preparing in all three of these areas will put you in a winning position before you even pick up the phone.

Key Takeaways

Identify and hyperfocus on the industries that are most likely to use your offer. When you niche down, you can craft hyper-personalized conversion conversations to your perfect prospect avatar.

Use a tight and refined customer-centric sales process. This could lead to increasing your income $50–100K+ this year without working harder or making thousands of cold calls.

What's the common theme of the tips presented in this chapter? *Time.* They emphasize the value of time and they bring you more of it.

You can't create more time, so you need to maximize the time that you have. When you look at a rep who is earning $500K–$1M+ a year, they have the exact same amount of time as someone making $50K a year.

The easiest way to maximize the time you have is to decrease the amount of time it takes to achieve something. It's about being wildly efficient with your sales process to gain back time.

Before you even begin to try to close your next deal, first write down your answers to the following questions:

- Do you know the best methods to do proper research on your target market?

- Do you have proven frameworks for cold calling, emailing, DMing, and social selling that leads to booked appointments?

- Do you know exactly what are the most important income-producing activities you must be doing every single day to get the results you want?

- Do you know the exact routine you should implement to be a top performer?

- Do you know exactly how to ask all the questions to effectively guide a sales process to move forward or to close?

- Do you have proven frameworks to present massive value and to destroy objections?

- Do you know the fastest ways to shorten your sales cycle?

- Do you know exactly what to do to deliver results without just working harder?

Get crystal-clear on who your ideal customer is, then prospect those first.

Think:

- What do my ideal customers have in common?

- What are their common characteristics?

- What makes them ideal?

- What industries are they in?

- What size is their business?

- What are some common psychographics?

- What are their needs, wants, and desires?

- What do they secretly fear?

After working with thousands of top-performing reps, this is actually a very common focus of the top 1%: They know their target market inside and out.

The top 1% are hyper-targeted with prospecting. Rather than trying to chase unqualified leads, they spend their time, energy, and effort selling to qualified prospects, dramatically impacting their bottom line.

Remember, the riches are in the niches.

SECTION THREE

How to Prospect Like a Bad@$$ Sales Expert

Rejection and mistakes teach you lessons that success will never teach you.

Getting Along with Most People Isn't Enough

When I got started in B2B sales in 2007, I thought sales would be easy since I got along with most people.

What I learned quickly was that the HARDEST part of B2B sales was prospecting—getting in front of enough qualified decision-makers every week! It didn't matter if I was a good presenter or not if I couldn't even get a meeting with them.

I felt frustrated with my (lack of) results. Demotivated.

Fortunately, through tons of trial and error, along with investing a lot into my own development, I was able to figure it out. Once I mastered prospecting, I started mastering other parts of the process and eventually became a great closer, too.

This ultimately led to consistent and sustainable sales success every single year in every single role I've been in from an individual contributor up to leading organizations of 110+ employees.

In fact, I've been fortunate at this point to have taught thousands of people, and they have seen some cool success.

And there are countless other examples of those I've taught that have been able to:

- Increase their income an ADDITIONAL $50K–$100K+ each year

- Consistently exceed quota every month, quarter, and year

- Receive tons of company awards and recognition

- Get promoted as a result of their success

- Create financial freedom

- Reduce their stress while building bulletproof confidence

- Sell as a LEADER and not just another "salesperson"

- Be able to teach and train others in what they've learned that made them successful

- Truly HELP their customers and clients

- And so much more

It all started with getting past the gatekeepers, which is a huge hurdle. Most salespeople are willing to use a script to accomplish this, but once they are through it, many of them tell me that they aren't really a "script person." Instead, they'd rather wing it with the decision-maker so they don't sound like a robot.

But remember this: If you aren't getting the results you want, then you need to do something different. And that something may be a script. As I mentioned in Section 2, *a script is simply a framework for success.* If you don't want to sound like a robot, add your personality to it and practice, practice, practice until it comes naturally.

Know the Purpose of Your Call

Before you pick up the phone, be sure that you are crystal clear about your objective for the call because that will determine how you write out your script. It is shocking how many people are unclear or their script doesn't match their objective.

Why are you calling?

- To book an appointment?

- To gather information?

- To qualify a prospect?

- To sell your product?

If you are calling to book an appointment, don't be focused on selling the solution. This is a common mistake I often see. If your goal is to book an appointment, you should be focused on selling the appointment, and selling that decision-maker on why they should take the time to meet with you.

Your Unique Selling Proposition (USP)

Before you can write out an effective script, you need to understand your unique selling proposition (USP).

We help [target market] achieve [x result] through [our solution].

This is a script for your USP. It is designed to be simplistic. On the phone, you always want to keep things simple.

If the script is complex, your prospect may stop listening. If you confuse them, you lose them. Be direct. You need to get to the point of the call within the first 10–15 seconds.

You need six ingredients for a delicious script:

1. Keep it simple.

2. Be direct and to the point.

3. Drop some social proof.

4. Present your USP, including benefits.

5. Be assumptive and confident.

6. End with a closing question that aligns with the objective.

Here's an example:

> Hi [name of person calling], it's Marcus with [your company name]. Thanks for taking my call. The reason I'm calling is I'm currently working with [put in current customers you are working with in their area to

provide social proof]. I provide them with [your USP, including benefits]. I have to show you this program. How is [closing question that aligns with objective]?

This whole conversation took maybe 15 seconds. I approached it with confidence as if the prospect knew me. I didn't add fluff such as "How are you doing?" I got right to the point. Simple and direct. I then provided social proof with three references to other clients I was working with that would be familiar to them.

Now, let's say you want to qualify them. Here is an example for that.

Hi Lisa, it's Marcus with ABC Payroll Software. Thanks for taking my call. Hey, the reason I'm calling is I'm currently working with [names of current customers] and I provide them with [USP]. I'm quite confident this would be a great fit for you too! Do you have 32 seconds for me to ask you a few questions to see if it makes sense to set up a time to discuss in more detail?

What's important to understand is that it's not the exact words verbatim that make them work. It's the **psychology of keeping it brief, simple, and relevant to them.** It's being able to show within a few seconds that you are someone of value and that you get them. Here's another example using a permission-based opener (this is inspired by my good friend and world-class sales leader, Belal Batrawy):

Hey Lisa, it's Marcus with Venli. You're not expecting my call. Do you have a moment? I promise to be brief.

[permission granted]

Great. In chatting with dozens of other HR execs in the SAAS space on the west coast, one of the largest costs they are running into are increasing turnover costs in their sales departments, in which each turnover can easily cost up to $100K+, if not more.

How are you handling these increasing turnover costs and reducing turnover?

If you use these scripts you will get results, but it's like eating a cake without the icing. (It's not bad … but it can still be better.) If you want your cake to have that creamy, gooey, rich icing, here's what you do. Concentrate on these three things:

1. **Pace:** Have a good cadence. If you go too slow, they may jump in and interrupt you or hang up. If you go too fast, they won't be able to understand you.

2. **Attitude:** They can't see you, so your voice needs to convey enthusiasm, energy, and a positive attitude. Who wants to meet with a boring person? Not me! You must also show confidence and conviction as if you've made thousands of calls in the past. Confidence sells, insecurity does not.

3. **Inflection:** When I talk, I inflect certain words. This also impacts the tone. I convey confidence, not ego. I have pure belief in what I am doing and it comes across in my tone.

Humor is also a bonus if it's not forced. If you are naturally a funny person, then add in that humor. If that is awkward for you, don't force it. Ultimately, you must sound human and natural, and that is why it's key to practice until it flows melodically.

Handling Phone Objections Like a Bada$$

It doesn't matter how simple your script is or how much research you prepare. At the end of the day, you will still have objections.

Your ability to handle the objections will determine your success in booking the appointment.

First and foremost, you have to believe that your offer will be the solution to their problem. If you don't believe in your offer, they will hear it in the words you say and how you say them.

You should feel confused when someone has objections. Think of it like warm chocolate chip cookies right out of the oven. If someone tells you they don't like them, you would think they were crazy, right? Who doesn't like homemade chocolate chip cookies?

That is the way you should feel when someone has an objection. You should have impenetrable belief that your solution can solve their problem and as a result, their objection should seem unfounded to you. Don't be cocky about it, though. You want to convey confidence without ego.

With that said, prospects are going to have at least two to three objections that you will have to address, so be mentally prepared to shoot for several no's to get the appointment. The key is to be pleasantly persistent—not aggressively annoying.

What I've found over dozens of industries is that 98% of the time, most prospects have the same 6–8 objections to meet. If you know this, you can map out your responses accordingly.

Here's a perfect example:

During one of my early sessions of making lots of dials, I was receiving a ton of objections. I made a note of why each person said "NO." You can imagine that, after logging 160+ dials of "NO," you can get a pretty good idea of all the objections!

I started putting them into categories. After a while, it started to become quite clear that there were many ways to say the same objections.

I was getting objections such as:

- The economy is bad

- Not interested

- No budget/money

- Loyal to a current vendor

- Already have a program/vendor in place/switched to a new vendor

- Under an agreement

- No need

- Had a bad experience with your company in the past

But I want you to understand this: Those prospects have one goal in mind when they give you these objections. They want to get you off the phone. Whatever their objection is, what is really happening is you are fighting their status quo. You are asking them to make a change from what they are currently doing, and people are resistant to change.

The mistake most salespeople make is that they want to have a different response for every objection. You could do that if you really want to, but the problem is that once you are on the phone and they throw an objection at you, it's easy to blank out, right?

You want to minimize having to think on the spot by building a system that you can inject objections into.

We are going to start off with a pattern interrupt that I learned from one of my sales mentors when I was first getting started.

> Prospect: *The pandemic has hit us really hard and we are in a weird spot right now.*

> **Response #1:** *Hey, that's exactly why we need to meet. How is Thursday at 8?*

This totally throws them off. If they say yes, that's great. Book the appointment. If they say no, which is more likely as you usually will have 2 or 3 objections, then you go into #2, which is a version of "feel, felt, found."

> Prospect: *No, we just aren't interested.*

> **Response #2:** *Bobby Jones, the CRO over at Johnson Tech, said literally the same thing at first, but he reviewed our program and immediately switched right over to us. How's Thursday at 8?*

If it's still a no, no problem. Go on to #3.

> **Response #3:** *[prospect name], I believe in our software platform. I promise not to waste your time. If you*

don't like what we discuss after 30 seconds, you can call
me your favorite expletive and end the video call
immediately. How is Thursday at 8?

Usually, you will get them to laugh with this one, and about
80% of the time once you have gone through three "no's,"
many prospects are impressed that you aren't giving up and
they will book an appointment with you. As with everything
we discussed so far, *how* you say it is most important.

But sometimes you still get a no and have to go to #4. This one
only works if you are in a field territory that you actually visit.
If you aren't or your territory is too large, skip this one and go
to #5.

Response #4: *Tell you what. Let me at least drop by,*
introduce myself, and drop some info off. It will take
12 seconds. Can I come by around [time] on [day]?

Then you can at least pop in and introduce yourself. Most of
the time when you are face to face versus on the phone, people
are a bit nicer. It's harder to reject someone face to face.
Hopefully you are so funny, awesome, and charming that you
will then get more time to hang out with them or book an
appointment.

So if you can't stop by or if they tell you not to come by, go to
#5:

Response #5: *I obviously caught you at a bad time.*
How about I call you two weeks from now to see if the
timing is better then?

Then add a follow-up task in your CRM to call them in two

weeks. When you call them next, leverage the power of the Terminator Script, which you'll learn more about in the next section.

By using this framework, you can be very effective. Notice a few key points that are very critical in the process:

- I ended every single objection handling flow with a closing question—otherwise, they may interject with another objection.

- Inflection, authenticity, and passion are key. Remember: Robots don't book meetings. Humans do. (So sound human.)

- Be very mindful of your tone—don't be too aggressive. Be pleasantly persistent while maintaining an upbeat positive vibe.

I have taught this sales sequence for years, and I know it makes many salespeople uncomfortable. But remember: Everything you want lies outside your comfort zone. Your ability to do this well will help you book more appointments.

Just like your scripting from the gatekeeper to the decision-maker, you must practice and record yourself with these scripts as well. The more you do this, the better. Run through the entire sequence as if you have gotten five "no's."

I practiced this every day, and it helped me to book tons of appointments. I got to where I was able to book 8–10 appointments in 2–3 hours. Sometimes I would book seven appointments in an hour. It really works!

Hypnotist Script

Even after you go through your objection handling and scripts, you are still going to get some "no shows." To help reduce these and increase your closing ratio, here is an effective script to use. Once I started using this, my "no show" rate went down significantly.

> You: *I'm looking forward to seeing you at [date and time]. Also, aside from yourself, does anyone else need to be present to get the program going? [this is a qualifying statement].*
>
> *Ok, great! I'm looking forward to seeing you [date and time]. In case something pops up between now and then, let me give you my cell. Do you have a pen? It's Marcus with [name of your company] and my cell is [xxx-xxx-xxxx]. Again that is [xxx-xxx-xxxx]. If anything pops up between now and [date and time], give me a call. Hey, what's your email so I can send you a calendar invite as well for [date and time]. Perfect. See you [date and time].*

Notice here that I have said the date and time 5 times. Hopefully by repeating it that many times, it is burned into their memory. Make sure to pause as you go through this so they "digest" what you are saying. You have also given them your name again just in case they forgot it during the call. And by sending them an invite you can re-emphasize the appointment.

Supplemental Power Scripts

The Voicemail Framework That Gets a 70% Callback Rate

Getting the prospect's voicemail in sales is inevitable. Some salespeople leave voicemails and some don't.

I used to think voicemails didn't work, but that's because I was leaving voicemails like this:

> *"Hi Johnny, it's Marcus with XYZ Company! I was calling because I wanted to set up a time to meet to go over my JKL program that will give you Benefit 1, Benefit 2, and Benefit 3! Please call me back on my cell at xxx-xxx-xxxx. Thanks!"*

I would literally get a 1% callback rate if I was lucky. The thing was that I knew voicemails were absolutely vital. I knew that if I called 60 decision-makers and got in touch with only 10, the other 50 were still viable opportunities. I just needed them to call me back.

Then one day, I received a voicemail, and I immediately called them back after I listened to it. Once I was on the phone with them, it became clear they were a salesperson trying to get me to refinance my mortgage.

However, this got my gears turning: WHY did I want to call this person back? HOW did they do it? And more importantly, how could I use this technique to ethically get people to call me back?

Then it hit me. They didn't sound like a salesperson in the voicemail. Their tone was firm, direct, and urgent. It was also a short voicemail that was to the point but vague enough to incite curiosity. All those things combined made me want to call back.

So I started rewriting my voicemail script. I made it short and direct, and I referenced an existing client. I practiced it so I could mimic the same tone as the call I got.

I also leveraged the Law of Authority. I tested it the entire following week. And the result? 60% called me back. Since they were calling me, their guard was down, and I booked almost all of them as a result. What was also amazing was that if I missed their return call, I'd get a voicemail with their direct lines and cell numbers too.

Now I'm a firm believer that a voicemail must be left every single time.

But here's the thing. A certain methodology must be followed. We have gone through a lot of scripts and frameworks already, but this is one that I recommend you DO NOT CHANGE AT ALL. I have tweaked and tested this script until I got the highest callback rate possible.

Voicemail script (firm):

> Salesperson: *Hi John, it's Marcus. I'm calling in reference to [a current customer's company name]. Please call me back on my cell at [xxx-xxx-xxxx], again [xxx-xxx-xxxx]. Thank you.*

The tone is so, so important. It needs to be firm with a bit of urgency. I don't say, "I'm with [your company's name]." Only say, "It's [your name]."

This voicemail is maybe 10-15 seconds long, which is important because if a prospect sees a one-minute or two-minute voicemail on their phone, they are less likely to listen to it. This also transcribes easier on their phone and increases the chances they'll read it if they have that option on their phone.

Your voicemail must incite curiosity to get the prospect wanting to call you back.

If they don't call you back after a day or two, call them back and leave the exact same voicemail. Every single time you call, leave the same message until they call you back.

Pro Tip: It is helpful to have different numbers to call from to switch it up. You may have an autodialer that changes the numbers, or you could call from a landline and a cell phone. Another option is to get several phone numbers through Google Voice, which is free.

And when they do call you back, this is what you say:

> Salesperson: *Hi John. Thanks so much for calling me back. The reason I called is I'm actually with [your company name] and I work with [the company you referenced] providing them [solution] that helps them achieve [result/benefit].*
>
> *I'd love to show how I can help your company too. How's Thursday at 8?*

The reality is that they are usually thrown off by this response and may be more open to it. If they do have objections, no problem. You go into the objection-handling sequence you just learned.

The Terminator Script

If you were pushed to speak with the prospect at a later date, this is the script that you will use.

> Salesperson: *Hi Lisa! It's Marcus with [name of your company]. Thanks for taking my call.*
>
> *The reason I'm calling you today is that I spoke with you on [date] at [time] and you told me to call you back TODAY SPECIFICALLY [today's date] at [time] to set up a time to review my [service or product] to [help you achieve a specific desired result that your target market wants] like I did with [current customer], [current customer], and [current customer]. How's Thursday at 8 am?*

This is a powerful script because, if someone told you that you could call back on a certain date, they will want to honor their word. They will be amazed in general because most reps won't call back when they say they are going to. They will be blown away by how detailed and committed you are.

Referral Script

If someone within the company you are calling referred you to the prospect, then you want to use this script:

> Salesperson: *Hi Johnny. It's Marcus with [name of your company]. Thanks for taking my call.*
>
> *The reason I'm calling is because I was speaking with [referral's name] and they told me to get together with you to go over our [program/solution] that I'm currently doing with [current customer and [current*

customer] to *[help you achieve a specific desired result your target market wants].*

In order for this to be effective, the referral person that you are mentioning should be at a higher level in the company—someone who has some clout.

I used this when I was with one of my reps in Portland. We were doing physical cold calls and walked into a large coffee company. We had with us a phone list of the company's directory, and I saw that Mike was the CEO.

I picked up the phone and I called Mike. He came downstairs to meet us. I did a quick spiel to book an appointment. Mike thought it was very comical because he said no one really asks for the CEO, but he did say that the VP of Operations was the person we needed to talk to.

The VP wasn't in, so the next day I had my rep call him using this referral script, and he effortlessly booked that appointment. In fact, he closed the deal in a matter of weeks and made thousands of dollars on that account in a short period of time. The average rep would have taken 6–12 months to close that deal, but because of the internal referral and going to the highest level first, he closed it in three weeks.

Now that you have all these scripts and frameworks, you want to map them out and make them your own. Print out your scripts and post them on the wall of your office or work space.

Map out your objection handling sequences, but tweak them so that they fit your style and the way that you talk. Print them out in large font and post them visibly, like you are reading from a teleprompter.

Then practice, practice, practice until it flows naturally and you can say it with 100% confidence and unwavering conviction.

Know Your Numbers for Success

Just as we talked about the importance of knowing two ratios for prospecting, there are some numbers you want to evaluate so that you can meet or exceed your goals.

A really important one is your **closing ratio:** How many first meetings do you need to make before you close one deal? (To ensure we are defining this the same, a "meeting" here means the first discovery call with the prospect, in which you are doing a deep dive into their needs.) If it takes you four discovery calls with four different prospects to close one deal, that means you have a 25% closing ratio.

You also want to know how many dials it takes to book one new discovery call, which is your **booking ratio.**

Also, how many dials do you need to close your target goal for the week or the month?

Let me give you an example of how this works. Let's say you have a goal of 12 deals per month and your booking ratio is 10% (out of every 10 dials, you book one presentation).

12 deals x 4 Discovery Calls per deal x 10 dials per presentation = 480 dials

This is the minimum number of calls you need to make each month to reach your goal.

Now you need to calculate how many hours you will need to make those calls. If you are doing 10 calls per hour on average:

$$480 / 10 = 48 \text{ hours per month and}$$

$$48 / 4 = 12 \text{ hours per week}$$

So when you are building out your routine and setting up your calendar, you need to make sure that you build in enough time on the phones. (More on this later.)

To help with motivation, let's figure out how much you earn per dial. If you hit your target goal of 12 deals a month, let's say you earn $10K in commission.

$$\$10,000 / 480 \text{ dials} = \$20.83 \text{ per dial}$$

This gives you some perspective so you can work to increase the amount you earn per dial. This is critical because it helps you stay focused and helps you realize that you do make money every time you dial, as long as you are intentional with it.

Although this example is more transactional, you can use the same principles to work backward for larger opportunities as well. The point is to know your numbers and to set yourself up for long-term success.

Additional Best Practices for Phone Prospecting

If you have consistent routines, you have consistent results. Here are some additional best practices:

1. Practice, practice, practice. I keep saying this but it is so critical. You can make your scripts sound natural by practicing. Build muscle memory. Sharp prospects can sniff out BS quickly. Don't let a lack of practice be the reason you have an empty pipeline. This is 100% controllable by you.

2. Reflect confidence and passion when calling.

3. Leverage voice inflection to emphasize certain words and drive an additional impact. Your prospects can't see you on the phone and determine whether or not to listen to you based on how you sound.

4. Adopt a power pose. Stand like Superman or Superwoman with your hands on your waist before you get on the phone. Shoulders back, chest out, and head up. It sounds strange but you'll feel better doing it.

5. Smile! People can tell over the phone if you are happy and energetic.

6. Expend energy and recover energy. When you are focused on making calls, it is mentally tiring. You can burn a lot of energy, so you want to run a consistent phone-prospecting structure. For example, 50 minutes on, 10 minutes off. During those 10 minutes, do something different. Go for a quick walk, stretch, have a snack, get some fresh air. Do something to recover your energy.

7. Train your mind and keep your energy high.

8. Feed your high-performance engine with high-performance fuel. Make sure you are eating foods that give you energy and not foods that make you lethargic and sleepy.

9. Just do it! Nothing works if you don't put the work in.

Common Mistakes You Don't Want to Make

1. "I'm not a script person." Nobody thinks they are a script person, but it only sounds like a script if you don't practice. When you have the script down, then you can adjust on the spot depending on the prospect. It's simply a framework for success.

2. "I get better results just by emailing or dropping in." You need multiple ways to reach your prospects. If you focus on improving your phone game, you'll book more appointments. People make the mistake of just focusing on emails or dropping in because the phones are usually the hardest area to excel in. But when you excel on the phones, you will have a massive advantage over your competition.

Using Emails to Load Your Funnel

Emails are another tool to reach your prospects, and emailing is definitely important, but I want to offer a word of caution. If you depend only on emails to load your funnel, you run the risk of becoming a keyboard warrior.

Now, I realize that some companies promote using email sequences. They try to wear their prospect down with 8- to 12-step (or more) sequences to get them to book a meeting. But relying solely on this one method is a mistake.

The reason I don't like this type of methodology is, number one, it drains you. And number two, your success rate is not as high as you might think it is.

For example, a pretty good booking rate is 5–10% off cold emails.

Some might be good with that, but I'd much rather have 10 decision-makers answer my phone call, and then I book 9 or 10 of them. Booking 90–100% is much better than sending tons of emails to get a 10% booking rate. That's really tough.

Another reason I don't love email is that email is super one-sided. When you send that email off, even with a really well-crafted email, you cannot handle objections. You don't know what the prospect is thinking or what objections they might have until they choose to interact with you.

If you have a decent open rate, then that may mean you have a good subject line, or maybe it gets opened because they want to see what the email is about. But just because they open the email doesn't mean they're interested.

I prefer phone calls over emails because, over the phone, not only can you hear your prospect's tone of voice but they can also hear yours. You can have a two-way conversation. You can interact in real-time. You can handle objections. And you can get important details from the conversation.

Don't get me wrong, emails are still a vital part of the sales process, as you need different ways to communicate with a prospect, but nothing beats a phone call for booking meetings.

Writing a Quality Cold Email

Now, at the end of the day, you need to know how to write a good cold email. You still need this in your toolbox. Let's go through how you can write better emails that are more likely to get a response to book a meeting.

Crafting a Quality Email

1. It has to be personalized to the prospect like a friend is writing to them.

2. It has to be simple and easy to read. (Shoot for fewer than 100 words. The shorter, the better.)

3. It has to be mobile-friendly since the majority of people are going to be reading your emails via their cell phones. You can email yourself to test it.

4. It must be value-driven and relevant for them. Bonus points if you give away something that's free and irresistible to them that solves a problem or pain point. This will increase your open and response rates.

5. There must not be much risk to them whether it is time, money, or resources.

6. You must have a soft call to action at the end. (Use only *one* CTA, not multiple CTAs.)

It's key to continue to work on your copy skills because it's critical from a social selling perspective to understand that each line of copy makes them want to keep reading the next line.

It needs to start from when they first see the subject line in the inbox. You want them to think, *This feels personalized to me. I'm interested.* Remember, a majority of people have the settings on their phone set up so that they can see the subject line and the first two lines of the email. So those three lines are vital in hooking them in.

Every line beyond that must make them want to continue to read to the end where you have your call to action.

There are so many cool tools out there to help your email stand out. Video can be an awesome touch. There are software programs you can purchase that allow you to input video into your email which is incredibly powerful.

Now, a word of caution. If you do video, the video *must* be customized. It can't be something you film as a generic message and mass distribute. Tailor your message to your prospect and make it clear that it's made specifically for them.

Structure of an Email

Every single part of an email is vital. So let's break it down.

Subject line:

R: relevant

E: ego-driven

C: curious

Ideally, it's relevant to them specifically. It's ego-driven—if you can make them feel good about themselves, that's really powerful. Make them curious so they wonder, *Hmm, what's this all about?*

First lines:

That ties into the first line of your actual email, which also needs to be relevant, ego-driven, and curious so they are thinking, *Clearly this is written to me and is relevant. I feel good about this. And I'm kind of curious, what's this all about?*

Next, you want to add in some sort of connection or reference point that's relevant. Something that connects the dots on your first line and, ideally, something you researched that is specific to them. Maybe there's a common connection you have on LinkedIn or something along the same line.

Body copy:

Then you have to get right to the point: your intent and value for them. Why are you reaching out? What type of value do you have to offer them? Then a soft, zero-to-low risk call to action.

And that's it. You don't want a lengthy email. It has to be very quick to read and understand. Your messaging has to be on point.

Let me give you some examples. This was an email that was written to me that I immediately responded to:

> *Subject line: More gym time?*

Marcus, I'm guessing you spend hours each week manually captioning your videos, literally manually editing, typing in, and adjusting captions. The whole nine yards.

Notice that the salesperson did their homework on me. It caught my attention and is relevant to me, right? This is about me, and they know I like to work out. It also means they've seen my videos and they've seen that I caption videos. They know my pain. That's really important.

Notice the really simple language, nothing complex.

I've been working with entrepreneurs like you for five years now. I would like to help you caption and get your videos up faster for your audience.

Your videos will look even more professional and you will have more time to go lift heavy things at the gym.

I took your most recent one and made some changes that I think your audience will love, so check it out here. Is this something you'd be open to learning more about?

Either way, keep up the great content.

Kind regards,

This person took the time to grab one of my videos, made it look super awesome, and sent it. This is a really good email. It's personalized. It's all about me. They know my pain.

So that means when you're writing your copy, write it *for*

them. It's not a pitch. That email didn't say, "Hey Marcus, I can do this and I can do this." Instead, it was all about me.

Then they added in a very soft call to action, asking if I'd be open to learning more about what they do.

Let me give you another example:

> *Subject Line: INC 5000*
>
> *Hey John,*
>
> *Congrats on hitting #487 on the INC 5000 list as that is an amazing achievement since you started only 4 years ago!*
>
> *In chatting with other CEOs of fast-growing start-ups in the HRIS space, they're usually running into growing pains trying to recruit and hire the right talent.*
>
> *Got a few creative ideas to help.*
>
> *Open to chat?*
>
> *All the best,*
>
> *Marcus*

Same elements, very soft call to action.

Omni-Channel Approach

Today's decision-maker is harder than ever to reach, so you will probably have to use the omni-channel approach to be successful in reaching them.

You can't DM, call, shoot them an email, and video message them on LinkedIn all on the same day. I would be pissed if I was that prospect. But you also don't want to only use one channel. You don't want to call them every single day this week. That just doesn't make any sense.

You have to exercise emotional intelligence. Imagine if you are the prospect, how do you want to be prospected? If a salesperson hit you up eight different ways in one day, or they only have one approach and kept going after you the same way over and over, wouldn't you get frustrated or annoyed?

It's important to understand there is no "one size fits all." Don't just assume that because they are a certain ICP or target market, you can stick them into an automated sequence and have success consistently. I would much rather have you hunting with a sniper rifle than a shotgun.

We know that technology is constantly changing, so the types of channels will change as well. The key is you want to adapt to the changes and be open and flexible in how you communicate. Regardless of the type of channel, you must exercise strong emotional intelligence, and always see it from the other person's point of view.

You also need to be pleasantly persistent. That's really important. You can't just shoot them a few emails or make a couple of phone calls and then call it quits if you don't reach them. Pleasant persistence pays off—especially with qualified prospects.

Customization is key. In today's time, tech has allowed us to use automation to scale our outbound efforts, but at the same time, prospects are tired of mass messages. Therefore, you must be able to stand out.

The more customized your communications are, the better, from your emails to your calls, to your videos, to text messages, to DMs. That's how you can gain attention and trust faster. Be different amidst all the templated messages everyone sends out.

Be sure you stay organized. Some people have software, and the CRM helps manage all of it. But if you don't, you want to make sure you stay organized, so let me go through some example channels from an outreach perspective.

The first day you call them, you leave a voicemail. The next day, you can drop a video DM via LinkedIn. The day after that, you can comment on their post. The day after that, you can shoot them an email. Notice that I'm switching it up, varying my communication channels.

Another sequence could be that I start with warming them up via social media by commenting on their posts, engaging with them, creating content to nurture them for a relationship and to show domain authority. Then I would add them on LinkedIn and eventually do the outreach.

There are so many different ways you could do this. Those are just a few examples. Vary your approach based on your sales cycle.

Consistent Prospecting Helps You Avoid "Commission Breath"

Prospecting is a high value and high leverage activity. It's an income-producing activity, so it must be done. It takes preparation and practice to be a master at all methods. Those who thrive are those who know how to prospect, and they do it consistently, so they don't go through rollercoasters of results.

On the flip side, the salespeople who have up and down months, quarters, and years and never seem to have consistency with their income have the same issue: inconsistent prospecting.

Inconsistent prospecting leads to a light pipeline, which ultimately detracts sales confidence and leads to feast-or-famine months.

You never want to end up panting as you near the end of a month. Believe me, when you're hungry for the sale to fulfill a quota, your prospect can smell it on you. You might inadvertently repel the existing opportunities in your pipeline with your "commission breath."

To have a thriving career in sales (and avoid dry months), make sure prospecting is part of your cadence as you run your weekly routine.

Key Takeaways

Think about this ... Have you ever seen a consistent, top-performing salesperson who wasn't confident? I'm not talking about ego or arrogance, but pure confidence and swagger.

This doesn't have to be an "in your face," gregarious personality. Some of the top professionals I know have a quiet confidence. It doesn't matter if you are an introvert or an extrovert. It only matters if you have a winning mindset and beliefs.

Here are some of them:

- I am in complete control of my destiny.

- I can control only what I can control.

- I do not sell products and services. I solve problems and offer solutions.

- My solution is a no-brainer. I have absolute belief that my solution is the best.

- I have the only cure to solve their ailment. Maybe or no are not options.

- I can't comprehend why they would not say yes today.

It is so critical to begin with the end in mind. When you have undying conviction that your solution is the absolute best, you end up solving problems for your prospects. Seeing them succeed creates bulletproof confidence in your offer. As you develop a top 1% winning mindset, your ongoing success becomes inevitable as it then flows through your entire sales process from prospecting all the way through the close.

What Happens When You Lack Confidence

Early on in my career, I was getting shut down constantly by prospects. I would get them on the phone, and I would go into a whole monologue about how great our company was, spouting off all of the features and benefits of our products. I would go on for 45–60 seconds, and inevitably (when they could get a word in) they would say they weren't interested and hang up.

That happened for the longest time. I was just winging these calls without any real structure, so even though I really wanted to get better, I wasn't succeeding. And with each rejection, I'd carry that deflated energy into the next call. As I continued to make calls, I could hear the insecurity in my voice increase as my confidence decreased because I wasn't having success.

It took a lot of rejection, but I FINALLY figured out some of the concepts I'm going to share with you here. For example, I figured out that I had to get to the point faster, my message needed to be specific to the prospect, and the biggest "Aha!" of all: I had to sound confident.

SECTION FOUR

Becoming a Guru
at Social Selling

---

*If you want something you've never had, you
must be willing to do something
you've never done.*
—Thomas Jefferson

Secrets to Selling Online

Let's say you're trying to sell video game controllers, gaming
systems, or any type of digital product. You'll want to go where
your customers are hanging out, right? It would be silly to try
to sell them at a countryside farm co-op where farm animals
and equipment are being sold.

You must go where your target market is!

Over the years, I've discovered that the LinkedIn social plat-
form is where my ideal prospects tend to hang out. In the past,
I've used LinkedIn as a tool to get a job, recruit, and get deals.
More recently, I've used it to build my current business, and
I'm going to teach you the strategies I used to generate a 7-
figure business in a short period of time.

Regardless of the platform, social selling rules apply. This type of selling is very different from face-to-face selling. You can use these concepts on any platform in the future.

It's important to understand that when social media is used properly, you can use it to generate inbound and outbound mouthwatering leads to close. And it can also be used as a powerful tool to nurture and build trust with your prospects.

But what if you're telling yourself one of the four biggest false beliefs around social selling? If you are, then you are definitely not alone. These three objections come up over and over again, and they're the biggest reasons so many salespeople are afraid to sell online (which gives you a massive advantage when you overcome them).

The 4 Most Common Objections to Social Selling

"Social Media Doesn't Work."

Social media is simply a tool. Any tool when used improperly won't be as effective as you'd like. It's like trying to hammer a nail with the opposite end. It won't work. But if you make a slight adjustment and use the right end, it works great. The goal of this section is to show you how to use the tool properly so you can get results.

"I Need to Post Every Day."

Unless you are trying to build a personal brand, you don't need to post daily. If you're planning to post, we'll cover some strategies in this section as well.

"Only 'Influencers' or 'Online Personalities' Can Get Meetings."

This is definitely not the case. You do not have to be an influencer or an online personality to get meetings and close. Even before I started my business, I was able to book and close meetings off LinkedIn with only a few hundred followers. A few *hundred*. Not a few thousand or tens of thousands. You only need to leverage the connections you make in a way that is sincere and helpful. People are interested in whether or not you can help them, not whether or not you have a big social following.

"But I'm Not Wired That Way."

Show me that there is something hardwired into your DNA that explicitly prevents you from using social media to sell, and I'll send you $100. I'm being facetious here, but you get my point. It might be new and uncomfortable, but remember: nothing great is built inside comfort zones.

As long as you know the top five rules for social selling, you'll find that it's a goldmine for getting meetings and closing sales. You just have to go about social selling the right way.

The Top 5 Rules to Social Selling the Right Way

Rule #1: Don't be spammy.

Don't cold direct message people asking for a booking or give them a spam pitch. That also goes for posting. Don't say, "Come book a time with me." That's not the correct strategy.

That's an example of really bad social selling.

People get annoyed by this, and it doesn't work. It also means people might develop a negative perception of you, which you definitely don't want. You do want to be sure that you bring value to your social media with the content you post, the comments you make, and your direct messaging (DMs).

Rule #2: Create content for your ICP.

If you're planning to post content, it's so important that the content you create and post is geared to your target market. And here's one that might surprise you: you want to give away 90% of your stuff. It will come back at least 10X. You are in this for the long game, and you want to build strong social trust.

Rule #3: Spend time where your people are.

If you think of all the social media platforms—LinkedIn, Facebook, Instagram, and many others—it's a big ocean for each of them.

Within each of these oceans, there are little bodies of water where YOUR people hang out. You may find them on several platforms, but find the one where most of them live. The bigger the platform, the harder they may be to find, so you have to be strategic about it. Find the oceans, find the smaller bodies of water, and then go fishing.

Rule #4: Engage in social selling daily.

Engaging in social selling daily is like eating healthy. If you only eat healthy food one day a week, you probably won't see results. But if you make healthy choices on a consistent basis, you are much more likely to get the results you are looking for. Daily interactions will lead to the kind of impact you want.

Rule #5: Use social selling as a tool to load your funnel.

If you use social selling in conjunction with cold calling, e-mails, door-to-door, mailers, or whatever ways you use to get in contact with prospects, it can supercharge your funnel.

In social selling, you want to focus on being someone of value —an expert. You'll spend more time upfront because you are new, and people don't know who you are. But if you keep delivering value, word will spread because of the great, consistent content you are delivering to your target market. And then they will start coming to you. When people see you as an expert, you become their go-to person, and you will generate leads.

How Social Selling Works

When we talk about social selling, there are two important strategies: inbound and outbound prospecting. With inbound prospecting, you attract warm leads based on your content. In outbound prospecting, you are looking for leads and actively starting new conversations. This is something you could start working on right now to generate your pipeline. You really want to have both types, which means you have to play the long game.

Six Steps I Use to Sell on LinkedIn

I personally like LinkedIn because it allows me to effectively do outbound and inbound strategies because of the way it's designed. I can find hyper-qualified prospects easily and can target them with outbound messages while also using content as a tool to nurture prospects and generate inbound leads. In the following sections, I cover specifically how I do it and how you can too.

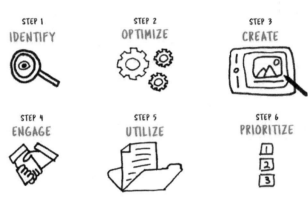

6 STEPS TO SELL ON LINKEDIN

STEP 1
IDENTIFY

STEP 2
OPTIMIZE

STEP 3
CREATE

STEP 4
ENGAGE

STEP 5
UTILIZE

STEP 6
PRIORITIZE

Step 1: Identify Your Target Market & Research

By now, I hope you know who your target market is. Next, you want to map out exactly the biggest problems they are facing or what would be most interesting to them that aligns with how your solution can help.

When you are doing research, these are the questions you want to answer:

- What type of content does your target audience engage with?

- What groups are they in?

- What questions are they asking?

- What comments are they making?

- Who are they engaging with?

- What's most important to them?

Here is a really powerful research hack. In any given industry, the target audience is going to have certain books and authors that resonate with them. So you can go on Amazon, find the book, and look at the reviews. You want to focus on the two-to-four-star reviews because those are the people who are posting questions or comments on what they like and don't like about the content. This will give you clues about your audience and what interests them and things they want to know more about. This is very powerful research for your content and your strategy.

For my market, which is B2B sales professionals, I might look up Jeb Blount's book *Fanatical Prospecting*. I can look at the reviews with two to four stars, and I can see the areas that Jeb missed in his book. And then I could fulfill them with my content.

Another research hack you can ethically steal from this book is to picture LinkedIn as a massive ocean. Ask yourself, *Where are my fish swimming?*

Let's say, for example, that you're targeting IT directors. First, you would search IT groups on LinkedIn. Now let's assume that there are 17K+ groups for information technology. Next, you want to look for the ones that make sense for your industry or what you are targeting.

I looked up the hashtag for information security on LinkedIn, and there are 3.6 million people following that hashtag. Chances are pretty good that some of the target market in the above example are following these hashtags as well.

As you are researching hashtags, micro and macro influencers, posts, comments, and Amazon reviews, make a list of all the themes, pain points, questions, problems, and concepts that you discover.

Step 2: Optimize Your Profile

This step is super important because once someone finds you on a social platform, the first thing they want to do is check you out. They want to know if they can trust you and if you know what you are talking about.

When optimizing your profile, think about what information will be interesting to your target audience. Position yourself as an expert, as a person of value. From all the research you have done, you know some keywords or vocabulary you can incorporate.

Your profile acts as bait for your prospect. All of it—your tagline, profile photo, backdrop, banner, summary, experience, recommendations, and the content you create—all aspects of your profile should be attractive.

As I explain the various sections of a profile, you might want to pull up my LinkedIn profile to see an example: linkedin.com/in/marcuschanmba

Tagline

Starting with your tagline, don't put something generic. I have a simple template—fill in the blanks:

I help _____ achieve_____
through _____ programs.

And here's a little hack. If you use an Apple device such as an iPhone to edit your tagline, it actually gives you more text space.

Profile Photo

Your photo should match what your target market wants to see. You want to look professional but relatable. Something that catches the eye and shows your personality.

Banner

Your banner at the top of the page is your billboard. It should be attractive to your target market and include a call to action. You can create a free one with available templates, or you can create your own by getting the current dimensions off the LinkedIn site.

"About" Section

If your prospect is still on the fence about you, they may go into your "About" section to find out more about you. Include your expertise and your story. People love stories. In mine, I included my accomplishments and some free resources. Everything in there is added to attract my target market.

Be sure that you are writing in simplistic words, usually at a fifth-grade level or below (you can use Hemingwayapp.com to help with this). You want your content to be easy to understand and digest, which makes it more likely that a prospect will actually read it.

"Expertise" Section

If they keep scrolling down, prospects will come to the section on your expertise. On mine, I wrote some more of my background (remember, people love stories), my accomplishments, and some free resources. I want them to relate to me and think, *Wow, this guy is achieving what I want to achieve. This person can definitely help me out. He is of value to me.*

Recommendations

Let's say they scroll through your experience, but they're still kind of on the fence about you. This is where it's really key to include recommendations. Your past customers can provide proof.

Again, this is all bait to track your target market. Your target market wants to know that you can really help them.

If they keep scrolling down your page, they might look at some of your content. You want to consistently create content that speaks to your audience. You want to be able to show that you can solve problems, provide tips and best practices, and be of value.

If you do it right, this can be a very powerful reach as long as the post connects with the audience, so this is a really quick way to build your brand.

BONUS TIP

Each social media platform may not have all of these components but they will have some or at least variations of them. LinkedIn also constantly comes out with new features or changes its capabilities. You can still use the same base principles we discussed above to stand out, gain credibility with your target market, and generate leads for your pipeline.

Step 3: Create Content

When we talk about content, let's discuss the types and themes to post on LinkedIn. You can do text only, videos, articles, and PDF slideshows, but ultimately, regardless of the format you use, the theme has to solve problems and be of value.

Your content can be written as a story, provide tips or resources, or be inspirational. Being consistent is the key, so I recommend setting up a schedule for posts.

Personally, I like to only post during business days for the most part. Now, some days if I have a promo going, I'll post on weekends as well for additional views. There's always good engagement then, but I primarily do five business days. So I have about 20 to 23 posts per month. I usually plan about a month in advance as this helps me minimize stress levels.

Key Content Posting Tips

1. Post every day on a schedule that fits you.

2. Provide value.

3. No spamming. No hard pitching.

4. Follow the 90/10 rule: 90% of your content is free, 10% is the promo.

If you simply do steps 1–3, you'll see inbound leads come your way and you'll make more connections with people in your target market.

If you're planning on leveraging content as part of your sales strategy, you need to understand how to engage with your prospects when you post your content.

Step 4: Engage with the Content

- Be sure to carve out at least 30 minutes per day to engage with potential prospects. You are investing this time in the long game, so be intentional with why you are on there. This isn't just 30 minutes on LinkedIn or another social media platform, this is actual time spent engaging with potential prospects.

- 15-20 minutes after you post content, be sure to go back on the site and engage every person who commented on your post.

- Comment meaningfully to build relationships. If they comment on your post, you do not want to ask them to DM you for more information. You want to make it soft and easy and have a conversation among your prospects. Engaging with your audience will give people a chance to like and trust you, and they will be more open to spending money with you.

- Find groups that align with your target market's interests and engage with the group members.

- Find large influencers or competitors in your space and engage with your prospects there.

- Find and use hashtags, commenting, liking, and engaging.

- No spamming—only post value and be helpful.

When I started my LinkedIn journey in 2019, I had about 3,500 followers. I ran all of these strategies I am mentioning here, and in about six months, I had over 10K followers organically.

Step 5: Utilize Inbound Prospecting

Inbound prospecting is when people are reaching out to you. As long as you are providing value for your target audience, you'll see them start to add and connect with you.

Once they have connected with you, it's a great opportunity to open a conversation with them. Follow these steps (in order):

1. Accept their request.

2. Send a customized video message. I'll also include a text message.

3. Provide them free value.

4. Include a soft call to action.

5. No pitch—start a conversation.

Your message breakdown:

- Start off with gratitude or a common bond.

- Get right to the point by sharing your reason for reaching out.

- Include a soft call to action.

They just have to click a button to see the video. It should be no more than 30 seconds. This is your first impression so you want your tone to be friendly and enthusiastic. This is an opportunity to connect with them.

The deposit:

You want to give them something free *that is of value to them.* Something impactful and easy to digest. This is key! For example, it could be an article you wrote or a free training. Here's an example script for the video:

> *Hey John! Marcus here. I just want to say thank you so much for accepting my invite. I really appreciate it. I loved your posts about [specific topics]. My goal is to bring massive value to CROs and I put together a short*

guide on 3 Tips to 2X Your Revenue Targets Without Increasing Headcount. I hope you find it helpful and I'd love to hear your thoughts. Take care!

If your company has something you can use, that is great. If they don't, I would suggest taking the time and possibly investing to create something. Once you have it, you can use it over and over again. If you need ideas, go back to the research we talked about earlier for your target audience.

Open the door to a conversation and keep offering value via your network. If you don't hear back from your prospect, you can follow up in 3–4 days. I like to drop a voice memo to find out their thoughts on the free value.

BONUS TIP

Using voice memos in the messenger inbox on LinkedIn and other social media platforms is another powerful way to engage with your potential prospects. This allows them to hear your personality, tonality, attitude, etc., which helps build trust faster. Use this simple strategy in conjunction with the others we've covered to help progress conversations further to book more meetings.

Step 6: Prioritize Outbound Prospecting

This is the process where you are reaching out to cold prospects that did not add you. You are on the hunt, and this is what you want to do to get new prospects.

You can do this on a basic LinkedIn account. First, identify a target prospect that you might find from comments, hashtags, or groups. You want to send them a message with the goal of starting a conversation.

Your goal is to open the door to a phone call or meeting. It has to be a soft approach. I'm going to share with you that my #1 method for a cold DM is what you read about in Step 5. The difference is that when you send the connection request, leave the body blank. You will see a faster acceptance rate this way.

Once they accept your request, you can film and record a video similar to the one you did in Step 5.

If you don't have a deposit to offer them, you can do a soft call to action. You won't get as high of a response rate but if it's relevant to them, you'll still stand out better than a templated copy and paste message. Here's an example script:

> *Hey John! Marcus here. I just want to say thank you so much for accepting my invite. I really appreciate it. I loved your posts about [specific topics]. The reason I reached out is that I've been working with 8 different CROs in the manufacturing space and have a few different ideas on how to 2X your revenue targets without increasing headcount this year. Would you be horribly opposed to chatting more about this? No worries either way. Just let me know. Take care!*

Like everything we discussed so far, HOW you do it is far more important than the exact words. Bring the energy, confidence, and conviction, and watch your calendar fill up.

Additional Social Selling Strategies

If you aren't connected with a prospect and they engage with your posts or check out your profile, connect with them. That's a warmup opportunity. If they are checking out your profile, you could probably do something of value for them.

Connect with them and then do the outbound messaging strategy. I'd also follow leaders in the companies you are targeting to gain insight, which can help with your messaging.

Have a cadence to follow. Don't just post a DM once and move on. The fortune really is in the follow-up.

Key Takeaways

- Spend time where your target market hangs out.

- Establish yourself as an expert in your industry.

- If you post, do it on a schedule that fits you.

- Make sure you engage.

- Do not spam at all, whether in your comments, messaging, or posts.

- Use your messages as a conversation opener and then shift to a phone call.

- Use social selling as a tool to help you accelerate the sales process and as another medium to get in front of your prospects.

SECTION FIVE

Preparing for the Initial Discovery Call

Success occurs when opportunity meets preparation.

—Zig Ziglar

The Separation Is in the Preparation

Let's review your journey so far. You've found a great prospect and you've booked a discovery meeting. Now it's time to prepare. The more prepared you are, the more professional you look, which will help to gain their trust more quickly.

Preparation is vital because it allows you to gain insight into the process before your actual presentation or meeting.

Remember back in school, if you had a presentation and you didn't prepare for it, you probably didn't have as much confidence in yourself as when you spent time researching and practicing what you were going to say.

Preparing gives you time to build a selling strategy. Setting your mindset up for success gives you the highest likelihood of being successful.

A large part of the preparation process is understanding how people psychologically process information.

There was a rep I hired years ago who was super high-energy like me. That's just how he was built and so he sold with a high level of enthusiasm. He did well, he was in the top 30%, but he sold this way to every single prospect.

When he was in a one-on-one meeting, exuding this high energy with a very reserved decision-maker, some became turned off by his personality and energy.

I saw how powerful and skilled he was, so I started teaching him how to shift his selling to the prospect's personality type. He increased his closing ratio and gained trust faster. As a result, he became #1 that year out of 300+ salespeople.

Identifying Your Prospect's Personality Type

According to Merrill-Reid's personality model, there are four basic personality types to identify so you can adjust your style to effectively sell to each one. You want to place every decision-maker into one of these four categories. Most people will be a blend of these, but they will have dominant traits to push them into one category over another.

Type 1: Analytical

These people are very detailed. They want all the facts, they may be highly critical and pessimistic. They are very perceptive and sharp. They like data displayed on charts and pie graphs. They want to check every option and they often will price shop.

This is how you quickly identify this personality type. When you walk into their office or see their background on a video call, this is what you might see: Their office is very neat, their desk is clean, they are probably conservatively dressed. Usually, they are on time, prepared, and very detailed. They are all business but at an unhurried pace.

Again, these are generalizations. They may not have all these traits but this gives you an overview.

Selling to an Analytical Decision-Maker:

You want to be extremely professional. Be sure you can back up everything that you say—no fluff. It's best to give a detailed, formal proposal using words such as precise, tested, and qualified.

These people don't usually like small talk. Read their body language and their eyes. If they look like they are getting annoyed, get to the point instead of trying to build too much rapport.

Don't give them too many options. Since they are analytical, if you give them too many options and selections, they will be overwhelmed and will need more time to process. If you confuse them, you lose them.

Don't use phrases like "This program is the best," or "It's amazing." These are too general for the analytical person.

Type 2: Driver

Drivers are objective-focused. Don't use fluff, get to the point quickly. They typically do not avoid conflict and may even enjoy it. They can come off as inconsiderate and blunt.

How to identify this group? They may seem rude upon intro-duction and come on strong, looking for a response. They may be impatient and impulsive. They may do two things at once while listening to you, and they may interrupt you.

Selling to a Driver:

When selling to them, give them a verbal agenda with a short, to-the-point introduction so they know what's going to hap-pen. Then, keep the presentation short and to the point.

Ask for their advice and ask closing questions. Be clear and direct with them as well, and do not waste their time sharing unnecessary details they did not ask for. Be efficient and meth-odical with your sales approach.

Type 3: Amiable

These types of decision-makers are usually very kind. They avoid conflict and have a difficult time making firm decisions. This can be very tricky if they are the primary decision-maker. They usually hate risk.

When you walk into their office, they usually have pictures of their family and/or pets. They may dress casually, perhaps even slightly sloppy. They may even come off as disorganized. They don't usually like change. They may be shy but open up if you ask the right questions.

It's really important that they trust you. They are relationship-oriented, so this can turn into a long sales cycle if you aren't careful.

Selling to Amiable types:

To sell to them, you need to develop a relationship with them and give them guarantees, as they don't like risk. Involve others in the process, as this additional input gives them safety.

It helps to put their mind at ease if you provide them with references and referrals. Don't push them too hard, they take their time. This doesn't mean you can't ask them some tough questions, but be cognizant of your tone and approach.

Don't talk only about business and don't show risk. If they think there is too much risk, they will get scared very quickly.

Type 4: Expressive

The expressive person is warm, enthusiastic, and usually a great communicator. They may be very competitive. They may like to exaggerate and they may lack some details. They want to be the hero.

When you walk into their office, they may have plaques, pictures, and awards displayed. They are fashionable and well dressed. They usually love to tell stories.

They may be interested in you and who you may know and how you can all be tied together, making those social connections.

Sometimes they talk in circles.

Selling to Expressive types:

To sell to them, you want to provide high-profile references and discuss some of your major accolades. They want to know that they are partnering up with someone great. Show them how your solution is going to make them a winner personally. Don't give them a lot of details and specs as it will bog them down. Keep the flow going, don't let them get bored during the process.

Ask for their help and expertise, and provide visuals.

Look for Clues

Now that you have a breakdown of these personality types, you can get a sense of their dominant type from your first contact with the prospect on the phone. You can also look at their online presence for clues: How are they writing, and what is their style? Do they even have an online presence? Are their answers short and direct? All of these things can help to give you an idea of the type of person you are going to meet.

This doesn't mean that you should walk in expecting a certain personality type and be prepared to sell that way, but it may give you clues.

But if their actions are totally different in person, then you need to be able to adjust your style.

Also, you may be able to put yourself in one of those categories based on your dominant traits. Being aware of this will allow you to adjust your style. For example, my dominant traits are driver traits. When selling to an amiable personality type, I must be careful not to overwhelm them or scare them off by being too direct.

How to Prepare for the Initial Discovery Call

I created an easy-to-use Discovery Call Planning Sheet. You can access it at **SixFigureSalesAcademy.com/prep.** It's a very simple digital sheet that you can use to prepare. It includes your selling strategy, the objective of the sales call, research on the company including the decision-makers, and questions you might use to guide the sales call. That way, it's all right there in front of you when you make the call.

At the top of the sheet, be sure to put down the prospect's name. Have you ever been on a call and forgotten the person's name along the way? Having their name written down is very powerful.

List your social proof—current client names that the prospect will identify with. This also acts as a reminder if you need to incorporate customer stories as part of your sales process.

Another important part is the customer pain points, as pain is what drives action.

This sheet is so powerful because it helps you stay organized. All of your info is in one place and you can use it to take notes during the conversation. The more time you dedicate to finding out key info, the better the call will go.

Research

To find out more about your prospect, look at the company website, their history, the "About" section, media press releases, and awards won. You want to find out what's important to them and what they focus on. Maybe there is some language that seems to keep showing up such as sustainability or safety and social responsibility for a manufacturer. If so, write them down.

Do a Google search to see what other details you can find on sites such as G2, Trustpilot, Glassdoor, Yelp, and Google reviews. You aren't looking them up just to see if they have bad reviews, although this is good to know. You also want to gain insight into what's going on with the company.

Check out all the social media platforms you can find including LinkedIn, Instagram, and Facebook. You can look up the company sites, but the decision-maker's personal sites may give you more insight.

For example, going to a corporation's LinkedIn site may just give you their generic info and their corporate copy. But by going to the decision-maker's page, you may find key things that they are personally connected with and very passionate about. There may be things that you see that you can personally connect with them on like some of their hobbies or a favorite sports team.

The point is that if their information is online, even a few minutes of searching and preparation can set you up ahead of the competition.

As you do your research, put key points on the sales sheet. Don't copy and paste all of their info, but pick out key points that you want to have in front of you.

What to Wear

I check my watch again: 9:40 am. I tap my pen impatiently on a pad of paper sitting on my desk as I check my calendar one more time. The entry is clear: *Ivan Dikiy interview, 9 am.* He was a referral from an employee at our company and we are understaffed, so I was cutting him some slack—but 40 minutes?

Just as I was about to give up on him, he strolls into my office in jeans and a polo shirt, sporting a beard. I'm sitting at my desk in a sharp suit with a tie, coat draped behind me on my chair.

His good friend referred him to me, so I know that he has to be aware of our dress code and clean shave policy. But he's here and we need good salespeople, so I decided to go through with the interview.

I ended up hiring him, finding out he was one of the most coachable people I had ever worked with, and he became one of the top reps in the company. (And one of the best dressed once he knew the expectations of the company culture.) But he almost lost his chance because he had not done his homework to find out about our culture. He was not prepared and it almost cost him an incredible opportunity.

You want to look the part for the sales call. The reality is that prospects will make a snap judgment from the very first time they see you, whether it's on video or in person. You only have one chance to make a first impression, so you might as well make it a great one.

Your company may dictate what you need to wear to a sales call such as a suit and tie, but if they don't, then figure out how people in that industry dress.

No matter what, always look professional. Treat it as if every detail about you will be scrutinized, whether you're following a strict dress code or dressing casually. Dress to impress but don't overdo it. Tiny details add up to either increase or decrease their trust in you.

How does your hair look? Are you well-groomed, from your facial hair to your fingernails? How do your clothes look? How do your shoes look? Are they in good condition? If you carry a briefcase, portfolio, or backpack, is it in good condition?

Are you setting up your visual image to match the value you want to deliver?

For instance, Ivan took the coaching to heart and his immaculate appearance went from beyond how he dressed to even how well-detailed and organized his car was. He knew as a field sales professional, prospects may potentially see the inside of his car, so he made sure it was spotless. Ivan also made sure that he had every sample possible in his car properly organized, in case he needed it to show a prospect to close. Ivan set himself up for success and he 100% looked the part.

Video Sales Call

Just like in an in-person sales call, dress professionally for the industry. You can get away with a dress shirt on top, and sweatpants (or hopefully some type of pants) on the bottom if they don't show. Whatever parts are visible should look professional. And be sure you don't need to stand up or go get something and have your sweatpants revealed!

Have a clean and visible background. It's better to have a real background than a virtual one. People may subconsciously wonder what you are hiding with a virtual background.

If you have limited space, be creative. You can hang a curtain behind you. I've seen people put up those Chinese folding screens, and it looks really nice.

Lighting is key: be sure you have bright lighting with minimal shadows. Have you ever been on a video call with someone who seems to be lurking in the dark?

Ideally, you want the light to either hit you directly in the face or at a 45-degree angle so you minimize shadows. Test your setting to be sure you look good. They sell inexpensive ring lights on Amazon if you feel like you need more lighting.

Be sure you test out the quality of your audio and video. The webcam on many computers is not the best quality, so you may want to spend a few hundred dollars to get a high-definition webcam so you can be seen clearly. Remember, a little psychology here: The better they can see and hear you, the more they are going to trust you.

Test your audio equipment to be sure that your prospects can hear you clearly. Some laptop computers don't have a good quality mic built in, so it may make sense to plug in earphones with a good microphone or invest in a good external USB mic.

Another tip: Be sure you look directly into the camera, not at your screen. Have you been on a Zoom call where the person doesn't ever seem to make eye contact and is looking all around? It's distracting. Also, be aware of where your camera height is raised. If it's level, they may be seeing your chin, which is not flattering. Raise the camera up to eye level or a little higher to get the visual perspective that you want others to see.

If you've noticed from all these small details, they are not anything crazy or hard to do. In fact, they are actually very simple...which also makes it simple to NOT DO. And most salespeople don't do them, so those that actually do automatically stand out in a good way and as a result, their win rate goes up too.

Overconfidence and Underpreparing

You book a call and you feel confident it's going to be a slam dunk. You feel like the conversation went well so you don't need to prepare. That's a huge mistake! The more intel you have on a prospect before you jump on a call with them, the better the call will go. One of the many fears a prospect has is that you will have zero idea about their business. By preparing in advance, you'll be able to eliminate any subconscious objections they may have. You are always better off over-preparing versus underpreparing.

Inconsistent Preparation

I've been with reps who say, "This account is only X size so we don't need to prepare." But the reality is that you really may not know everything about the potential of that company. Don't underestimate your prospects.

You may walk into that meeting, and it goes a different route and explodes into 10X the size you expected. The more prepared you are, the better you are going to look.

The separation truly is in the preparation, so be consistent and prepare for every single call.

SECTION SIX

How to Make Your Discovery Calls POWERFUL

Successful people ask better questions, and as a result, they get better answers.

—Tony Robbins

Apply the 90/10 Rule

Have you ever been on a date with someone who just wouldn't stop talking? Sitting across from your date, thinking you're going to have some great conversation over the crispy fried calamari that just arrived, you quickly realize that this is not a conversation at all. It's a show. And they're talking mostly about how awesome they are and what THEY are interested in.

When you're selling anything to anyone, it's absolutely vital to gain trust and credibility quickly. The best way to do that is to keep in mind the 90/10 rule: 90% is asking questions and 10% is presenting. Meaning, it's better to be INTERESTED than to be INTERESTING.

90/10 RULE

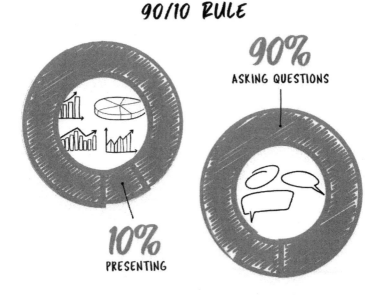

90%
ASKING QUESTIONS

10%
PRESENTING

The truth is that trust and likeability are more than likely limited between you and your prospect. Depending on how good you were on the phone, they may believe they have little or no need for your product or service. Especially if this was a cold outbound prospect that you cold called and you got three or four "nos" on, but you still got the appointment because of your persistence and sales skills.

In order to build that trust and likeability, there are six "must haves" to help you land the sale.

6 Things Every Sale Must Have

1. They must like you, at least to a certain degree, or else they will end the meeting.

2. They must trust you.

3. They must have a need.

4. They either have to be able to afford your product or service or be able to access the funds or resources to afford it.

5. They have to have an urgency to take action.

6. There must be minimal friction so it's easy to switch.

And if it's a complex sales process, meaning it involves multiple stakeholders, these still apply, or else the deal will stall out.

4 Steps to Mastering Your Discovery Calls

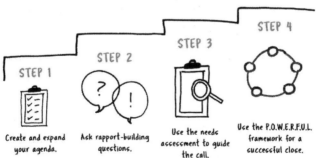

4 STEPS TO MASTERING YOUR DISCOVERY CALLS

STEP 1 — Create and expand your agenda.

STEP 2 — Ask rapport-building questions.

STEP 3 — Use the needs assessment to guide the call.

STEP 4 — Use the P.O.W.E.R.F.U.L. framework for a successful close.

Step 1: Create and Explain Your Agenda

Explain why you are there and your value proposition. Your value proposition:

- Lets the prospect know the agenda for the call

- Allows them to know you will ask for the business/sets the precedent

- Adds professionalism and gives you structure for the sales call

This works whether you are doing a video call or meeting face to face. Either way, you want to start with some small talk to break the ice. Once the small talk dies down, then you go into this sales call structure.

> *Ms. Prospect, thank you so much for your time today! Like I mentioned on the phone, I'm currently working with _____, _____, and _____ in your industry.*

So already in this short intro, you are stating their name, showing gratitude, and referencing back to your last connection point. In addition, you are giving them social proof. This is really similar to your phone script.

> *I've helped them with our demo software solution that has helped their sales teams double their closing ratios and ultimately hit their growth targets faster while helping reduce sales turnover drastically.*

So again, this is very similar to the phone script with the value proposition, and it's clear you know the problems they are running into and potential desired outcomes.

116

Next, you go through your agenda:

> *What I'd like to do today is ask you a few questions about your business to make sure I get a good understanding of it. If it makes sense, I'll then make you a few customized recommendations, and if it all sounds good, we will get you set up today. Sound good?*

Simple and to the point. And the more casual you can make it, the better. You told them what you are going to do, and you included a trial close at the end. You can take the same framework and adjust it to fit more transactional sales or even adjust it to fit large enterprise sales as well. The prospect will either agree, give you a maybe, or they may say, "I don't make these decisions, someone else in our company does."

If it's a transactional sales process and they aren't the decision-maker, I highly recommend you say, "Oh you know what? Can you grab [decision-maker] for this meeting? Or can we set up another time when they can join us?"

This is really important. You want the decision-maker to be there to shorten your sales cycle. If they say no, everything has to go through them first, then fine, move forward.

BONUS TIP

When prospecting, this is why it's key to start as high up as possible on the food chain. When you can get executive buy-in early on, it helps drive the rest of the sales process. This is especially key for large complex deals that span multiple buying influences.

Step 2: Ask Personal Rapport-Building Questions

At this point, you should have developed some logical trust with your prospect. You look professional, are well prepared, and have an agenda. So what you need to do now is develop some emotional trust by subtly getting to know them personally.

Ask them a personal question and listen attentively. Respond positively with good eye contact and open body language. Always be authentic and focus on making them feel good about themselves.

Remember to only ask a few questions, and make sure they are ones that will either help you gain trust or move the sales process forward. Don't ask questions just to ask questions or you will waste both your time and theirs. Control the conversation so you don't go down a rabbit hole and use up all your time.

So here's an example. After you make your trial close, you need a transition statement, something like this:

Ok, great. Before I get into that though ... How long have you been with/owned the company? How did you get started with this? What interested you about the industry?

Make sure you are listening and responding back to whatever they tell you in an authentic and positive way. Compliments can go a long way, especially if you weave in positive research you have found such as awards they have won.

Be cognizant of their time and yours. Don't spend too much

time in this area. If they don't see the value in spending time with you, your chances of securing another meeting go down. Just ask a few questions and then move on.

Step 3: Use the Needs Assessment to Guide the Call

The needs assessment section is all about your prospect. This is key. By following these steps, you will glean everything you need to know to close a prospect. In these steps, the goal is to ask questions that cover the goals of the business, their desires, why they buy, what are their reasons for making a purchasing decision, and any key technical specs that are required or desired.

How will your products and services align with their purchasing decision, and how will that align with the goals of the business? Are there any pain points they may have with their current vendor or provider?

Think of the needs assessment as a road trip you are setting off on. You are at Point A and you want to get to Point B, which you have never been to before. You don't want to start driving aimlessly and hope you eventually arrive—you want to ask the right questions to get you there.

So that's what you do with your needs assessment. Point B is a closed deal. What questions do you need to ask to get from Point A to that closed deal at Point B?

- What are the goals of the business? What does your prospect desire? People typically buy or invest for emotional reasons and then justify it with logic. Do they desire to make more money? Save money? Save time?

Retain customers? Avoid effort? Escape pain? Gain praise and recognition?

- Why do they buy? What benefits do they need? Some people buy to make their life easier. Other benefits might include convenience, cost savings, status, customer benefit, eco-friendly, etc.

Once you uncover the benefits they want, it must be crystal clear to them that your offer or solution will give them these benefits. It must be clear that your solution will lead to their desired benefits/problems solved which should lead to them achieving their core goals.

If they see that the offer gives them some benefits but they can't see how it helps them achieve their goals, it's unlikely you will get the deal.

For example, I think Lamborghinis are really cool, high-end supercars. If I were to buy a Lamborghini, I could picture myself looking pretty cool riding around in it. I would get a lot of benefit from having such a cool car.

However, it's really expensive. Since one of my goals with my business is making profits, there isn't a connection from the product (the Lamborghini) to helping me achieve the goals for my business. The Lamborghini would give me the benefit of looking cool but it doesn't help me achieve my goals. So that's why I don't have one.

Here's a more practical example. When I worked for a corporation, my team sold restroom supplies like paper towels, toilet paper, and soap. Our offer was to deliver the products, manage customer inventory, and make their lives easier.

We were able to show prospects that by choosing the restroom supplies option, they saved overall time (no more trips to the store or wasted time managing inventory and ordering), and they saved on costs (both hard and soft). They consolidated multiple vendors and achieved their goal of profitable business growth.

Here is a tip: if the prospect doesn't know the goals of the business, there's a high likelihood that they're not the right person to meet with.

The best way to handle any objection is to eliminate it before you ask for the business, so this becomes the most vital portion of your sales process.

You will find out fairly quickly that you will have almost the same objections every time, so become a master at handling them. The needs assessment or discovery, when properly done, arms you with the tools to handle and close any objection you encounter.

Step 4: Use the P.O.W.E.R.F.U.L. Framework for a Successful Close

When you do it like above, your discovery becomes POWER-FUL as it sets you up for the highest possible win rate. If it helps you remember it better, a phenomenal discovery will lead to you uncovering the following 8 beliefs that ultimately lead to a virtually objection-less close:

Pain—They 100% believe they have a big problem(s) that needs to be fixed.

Opportunity Cost and COI—They know there is a huge cost of inaction if the pain is not relieved.

Wants and Desires—They know the clear desired outcomes from solving the problem(s), big goals, initiatives, etc. at the micro and macro level.

Executive Level Influence—They know they have decision-making power and process and/or have leverage to help you with this.

Resources—They believe they have access to funds or more budget to implement the solution.

Fear of Failure—They have doubt and uncertainty regarding their existing situation/vendor, in that they can solve their big problem.

Unequivocal Trust—They have 100% trust in your company, product/service/solution, *you.*

Little Stuff—They are 100% certain that you can meet and exceed all the specifications for implementation.

The reason this P.O.W.E.R.F.U.L. framework works so effectively is that each letter represents different beliefs. So the questions you ask must be geared toward extracting and building up (or breaking down) these beliefs in the prospect's mind. Beliefs lead to actions being taken, which is exactly what you want your prospect to do.

If there are multiple buying influences in the process, then you must ensure each of them is also 100% certain on each belief so you can speed up your sales cycle. This way, you are gathering powerful intel that can set you up to win.

It's a lot like sports. The best teams in the world will review the past games of their competition to gather intel. They will learn the strengths and weaknesses of each team member and how they play. They'll identify patterns, trends, and commonly run plays, so they can try to predict what the other teams may do when they are playing against them.

They spend all the time upfront preparing and gathering intel so when they play, they can have the highest possible win rate. The more intel they gather, the more likely they are to be successful in running plays against them. It doesn't mean it's a guarantee, but when you have all the right intel upfront, it is so much easier to do.

Likewise in the discovery, when you ask the right questions and uncover the P.O.W.E.R.F.U.L. beliefs, it arms you with intel on how to now best present your solution to close the deal.

Important tip: do not pitch or present during this step.

This is all about the prospect. You may be tempted, but don't do it.

For instance, as you start to uncover their pain points, they may ask what your solution would be. You will be tempted to share it, but instead say something like, "Hey listen. I can't wait to share with you how I can help you solve this problem. Let me ask you a few more questions so I only share what's relevant and valuable for you. Sound good?"

If you do this right, it is not uncommon that by the time you finish your discovery, the prospect may be sold on you and your company, even if you have not presented a single thing.

Let me repeat that as it's so important: **if you do a great job upfront uncovering the goals and benefits the company is looking for, you can align your solution to tie those goals and benefits to it.**

> If you have downloaded the needs assessment discovery worksheet **(SixFigureSalesAcademy.com/discovery)**, you will see that steps 1–4 help you map out your core questions so you can get started in uncovering the P.O.W.E.R.F.U.L. components. Then you want to put all those questions into a sales call planning sheet.

Discovery Call Planning Sheet

A discovery call planning sheet is a very simple format that you can use to prepare for your calls. Write down everything so that you have all the information at a glance. Include the prospect's name, your social proof, and all of your research. Then start coming up with questions that you will use to guide the discovery call.

Some sample questions you might ask your prospect on uncovering pain:

- What made you reach out to begin with?

- What would you say right now is your biggest challenge?

- What makes you say that?

- What have you done so far to try to solve [issue]?

- For how long?

- How has it impacted you? Your team? Customers? The company?

- What do you think has been holding your team back from resolving this?

Ask one question at a time. Adjust the phrasing if needed so it sounds like your voice and style, and add context if needed. You will usually just want to ask a few of these, not all of them, as each question will lead to follow-up questions.

Here is an example:

> You: *What made you reach out to begin with?*

> Prospect: *We're looking to switch to a new sales CRM and are evaluating vendors.*

> You: *Got it. What's sparking you to look into this?* (Practice active listening to their answer.)

> Prospect: *We've been using Google Sheets to track it and we've outgrown it.*

> You: *Makes perfect sense. When you say "outgrown it," can you elaborate on that?*

Prospect: *It's very manual and tedious. Our reps have to go back and remember to update it as it's not syncing with our dialing software or email tools.*

The C.O.D.E. to Ethical Persuasion Tactics

Next, we are going to go deeper into the art of asking questions through ethical persuasion tactics. Here is the C.O.D.E. to ethically persuade your prospect:

C.O.D.E. TO
ETHICAL PERSUASION TACTICS

C	ONNECT
O	PEN
D	ECISION
E	XPAND

Connect: Open up your prospect by using questions to connect both logically and emotionally to give them the option to trust you and answer you.

Open: Use questions instead of statements, as questions make it a dialogue and it's about THEM versus you.

Decision: Allow the prospect to make a decision to answer and engage.

Expand: Expand the conversation with follow-up questions to go deep.

Active Listening

Your prospect is like an onion. Your questions are your knife. You need to keep peeling back the onion using questions to get to the core where people feel heard, understood, and connected.

In this place, they will be most likely to do what you are asking them to do. This doesn't just apply to sales; it also applies to leadership, relationships, and all areas of your life. This is the power of active listening.

I want you to look back at all those questions we went through. Believe it or not, they only peel back a few layers, so you need to go deeper. (You saw a little bit of that in the pain questions example from before). The fortune is in the follow-up questions.

The more questions you ask that allow you to go deeper, the more you get to the heart of the onion.

1. Ask open-ended questions.

2. Mirror/clarify with follow-up questions.

3. Repeat back what they said as a question for understanding.

So we already discussed some first-level questions. Once they answer, you want to mirror, or repeat back the last few words that they said and frame it as a question.

> You: *Where do you see your business going in the next 5 years?*

> Prospect: *We want to grow our business.*

> You: *Grow the business?*

Ask this in an inquisitive tone and then pause. It's important to pause after every question, listen, and wait.

> Prospect: *Yeah, we want to have 5 locations.*

> You: *Five locations?*

> Prospect: *Yeah, we want to have one in Florida, Alaska, Oregon, Washington, and Georgia.*

> You: *That's great. How are you going to get there?*

So this is mirroring to get deeper. You can also do clarifying which is the technique I personally use more often. It can be paired with mirroring or done on its own. Think of how, what, and why questions that are open-ended.

> You: *How are you going to expand into those locations?*

> Prospect: *What do you mean?*

> You: *It seems like it's really important to you. Why is that important to you? Tell me more.*

As you go deeper, be really cognizant of your tone. If you don't have the right tone, you can come across as if you are challenging or interrogating them, instead of just being inquisitive. Be authentic and real.

128

Then repeat back what they said for understanding and clarity.

> You: *Ok, Lisa. If I understand you, you want to grow the business to 5 new locations next year so that your parents can retire and not worry about their finances, is that right?*

This line of deeper questioning accomplishes several things. First, you can be sure you heard them correctly. Second, it may make them feel more heard so they will trust you more. And make sure you use their name.

This mirroring or clarifying doesn't have to be done for every question, but you definitely want to do it for the big goal and benefits questions, as this drives everything.

This simple strategy by itself will improve your ability to persuade ethically because you are becoming a master at asking questions and listening.

So in a perfect world, if you do an excellent job with this discovery process, the prospect is going to like you; trust you; know they have a clear, active need; feel the urgency to take action; and be salivating for your solution, even though they don't know what it is yet. Again, you should NOT present at this point. This is all about THEM and not about you.

At this point, you will know:

- Goals of their business and their desires

- Why they buy and what their reasons are for making a purchasing decision

- Any and all key technical specifications needed or desired

- How your product or service aligns with their purchasing decision

- How your product or service aligns with the goals of their business

- Any pain points or issues they may have with their current vendor

- Decision-making process

Ultimately, you know they are 100% certain for each of the P.O.W.E.R.F.U.L. beliefs. They fully believe and understand:

- There is a major pain or problem that must be solved.

- They know there is a large opportunity cost for not solving the problem (the cost of inaction).

- They have clarity around their wants and needs and how your solution will help them achieve the goals of their business. This could also include intrinsic or extrinsic personal desires.

- They believe they have executive-level influence to make a decision and/or they can influence others in the organization to make a buying decision.

- They believe they have the resources or access to funds to make this happen.

- They believe they have fear of failure, meaning they doubt what they are currently doing will get them to their desired outcome.

- They have unequivocal trust in the solution, your company, and you.

- They believe you are able to completely meet their needs for the little stuff—the specifications needed to fully implement your solution to help them solve their problems and help them achieve their goals.

This is where the sales call planning sheet is so important. Before you move on to presenting, make sure they have answered all your questions. If you missed an area, go back and dig deeper. If you didn't uncover all the goals and needs and you go on to present, it will be super awkward because you don't know what they want. You have to know what they want.

Recap and Transition After the Needs Assessment

Once you have achieved all the objectives of the needs assessment and discovery, you want to recap what you have learned with your prospect. This might be in the same meeting, or it might be a second or third, depending on the size of the deal and the parties involved.

> You: *So Lisa, to make sure I heard you properly, you told me that it's important to you that the software you use is easy to use, looks professional, and can grow with you because you are focused on growing your business, being more profitable, and ultimately saving yourself tons of time. And you are having these issues X, Y, and Z.*

This recap is very simple, but it ensures that you actually know what you are talking about and you understand their issues.

Next, you want to present your solution. This is your time to shine! Remember you want to present ONLY the features and benefits that are going to help them achieve their goals and desires and eliminate their problems. You also want to make sure to adjust the presentation to their personality type.

I also recommend that you use visuals as it makes it much more real and powerful for your prospect, tying it all back to their end goals and desires. The simpler you can do this, the better. Remember: If you confuse them, you'll lose them.

It must be as easy as possible for them to switch companies and do business with you. Remember we talked about removing the friction. Deal with anything upfront with your solution that could lead to a future objection. Here's your framework:

> You: *Earlier you told me [need/benefit] was important to you. On our solution, we have X feature that provides [benefit they mentioned]. This will help you achieve [goals/desires they mentioned].*

And here's an example in practice:

> You: *Earlier you told me that taking care of your employees is important to you. On our flexible spending account app, we have an auto-receipt upload feature that makes it super easy for your employees to use to upload medical receipts. This will make them super happy and ultimately lead to them helping your company grow.*

So in this example, I'm not just saying we have a flexible spending app, and I'm not just saying we have a receipt upload feature. I'm tying it back to their business and the fact that taking care of their employees is important to them. The benefits are that it's super easy to use, your employees will be happy, and they will help grow your business, which is one of their needs that they want to achieve.

After each agreement, make sure you trial close before going on to the next one. It sounds something like this:

> You: *Hey, can you see how this would help? This would solve [X problem], right? You see how this is better than what you are currently doing? How do you see this feature helping you?*

These types of trial closes are really critical because they allow you to gauge feedback and see what the prospect is thinking. If they are loving it, they'll tell you. If you sense they are not loving it, now is the time to dive in to clarify as you may have potentially missed something. You want to do this for every feature that makes sense to present. However, find a good balance. If you do it too many times, it'll come off salesy and robotic.

If you have done everything properly, by the time you are done presenting, chances are good that they will be salivating about your offer. You uncovered all their needs and you aligned everything.

They may or may not have asked about price. If they ask about price early on, it's OK to give them a wide range from the lowest to about 10% to 20% above your highest point.

The mistake that people make is either to tell them the price before they earn the opportunity or to push it off and say, "We'll talk about it later." But you can do it very simply.

> You: *Hey Lisa, great question. Our solutions range from $1,000 per month up to $50K per month, depending on which package you go with. As we go through the packages, I'll give you the exact specifics so you can make the best decision. Does that sound good?*

Framing Value Over Pricing

The law of relativity says that nothing has meaning without something to compare it to. Let's say you are in a meeting and it's time to present the pricing. You may need a few minutes to draw up the proposal for them, so you go out in the lobby, and they may take this time to go through their emails or return a phone call.

The reality is in that short amount of time, their mind will probably shift from being excited and in the right mind space to being wherever they went in that 5 or 10 minutes.

So you need to shift them back. This is especially important if you have had two or three meetings where you did the discovery process in the last meeting and now it's time for pricing.

If you start the meeting going right into the pricing, they've already forgotten every piece of value you presented to them in the previous meeting. So it's important that you open with some questions before you go over pricing. Here's what that could look like:

You: *Hey, pricing aside, what did you like most about what we've discussed so far?*

Let them tell you, and then ask, "What else?"

Get them to tell you as much as possible and then repeat it back to them, aligning with their goals. This is very powerful because it will help you help them to reconnect the dots between your solution and the goals and benefits they want to receive.

Guide them through with open-ended questions so that they remember all the benefits and features. This way they themselves are answering you and affirming what they like. This shifts them back into a different part of their brain where you can sum it all up and transition to your close.

SECTION SEVEN

How to Close Without Being Sleazy

To master selling is to serve at the highest possible level.

Salespeople are people who convince and fool poor customers into buying things they don't need. That's what I thought before I started in sales.

You see, here's the thing. People will resist what you tell them but never doubt what they conclude on their own.

There is definitely a specific mindset that you want to learn so that your closing is done properly and ethically. When you have asked the right questions upfront, you then earn the right to ask for the business. You want your mindset to be that this is the next part of the process.

Your body language and vocabulary must reflect a mindset that you are worth the price that you are asking for. You should not use any weak language. You must also have 100% certainty and belief that you have the solution to their problem.

This should all be super logical. You have uncovered a need and now you are offering a value-added solution. Don't over-complicate it—just ask for the business.

The Simple Close Framework

Simple close example A:

> *Ok great. So to provide you with my X solution that will give you A, B, and C benefits so that you can achieve D goal, it's only $____. Should we go ahead and get you set up?"*

Other phrasing options to use for the close:

- *Hey, should we get that paperwork taken care of?*

- *Let's get this set up, sound good?*

- *We just need to take care of the onboarding paperwork and we'll get started tomorrow, sound good?*

- *Should we go ahead and bring the product out next week?*

Look them in the eye, smile, and be quiet. Then wait for a response—this is the hardest part! STOP TALKING. Watch their eyes and their body language.

Some common rookie mistakes:

Mistake #1: Not following the 90/10 rule and talking too much. Remember: 90% asking, 10% presenting. Less is more and do not talk through the sale.

Mistake #2: Not earning the right to ask for the business.

At this point, they will either give you a yes, no, or maybe. If it's no or maybe, then they have objections, so you need to get those objections out so you can address them.

You can nail every part of the sales process, but if you can't handle objections, your results will be impacted.

I have found that there are a handful of common objections that happen across the board, no matter what industry you are selling to.

Common objections:

- I need to think about it.

- I need to check with whomever.

- It's too expensive.

- Let me compare it to another vendor.

- I don't see the value in it.

- I'm under an agreement with another vendor.

You will see variations of these, but the objections will almost always fall under one of these areas.

When they throw these objections at you, it doesn't mean that is their only objection. What they're saying may only scratch the surface of their concern. In other words, it may be a smoke-screen for what is really on their mind. Each objection can mean something totally different for each person.

For example, determining how expensive a restaurant is can be very subjective. One person could look at a $50 plate as too much, while another person thinks it's a deal for what they get.

There are steps to take to handle objections and I'm going to go through each one. Here is an overview of what these steps are in my H.E.A.R.T. framework:

1. Heard—Make them feel HEARD.

2. Elaborate—Have them ELABORATE on the objection.

3. Aside—ASIDE from the real objection, ensure there are no others.

4. Reclarify—RECLARIFY value and have them share what they do like.

5. Transition—TRANSITION them back to what has been discussed to show why the objection should not be an objection.

H.E.A.R.T. FRAMEWORK

H EARD

E LABORATE

A SIDE

R ECLARIFY

T RANSITION

When most reps get hit with an objection, they tend to jump in and try to oversell. They handle that surface-level objection and then they may get another and another. It feels like a ping-pong game. Back and forth. Objection, response.

The reality is that the first objection is almost always a smoke-screen. After you make them feel heard, you want to focus on getting the prospect to clarify and elaborate on the objection so you fully understand where they are coming from.

This is the most important step in handling objections. For instance, you can ask the prospect:

> You: *What about X concerns you?*

Wait until they tell you more.

> Prospect: *It's too expensive.*

> You: *I can appreciate that. What about X concerns you? Tell me more.*

You are trying to go deeper. They may tell you that they have a budget of $12K/month and your proposal is for $15K/month. They need to be able to justify going over budget. You may find that it isn't about price, it's actually about value, which is a totally different objection. Try going several layers deep so you can get to the core issue.

When they go deeper, you find out that your product is $5K/month more than their current vendor. They are willing to pay $2K/month more for your service, but they would need to justify the ROI for the extra $3K/month.

> You: *So aside from justifying the extra $3K per month, is there anything else holding you back?*

This is really important to ask because it will help to minimize future objections. If they say, "No, that's it," you want to clarify again by restating their objection.

Once you get an affirmative answer, you can go to step 4 to clarify the value.

> You: *Remind me again, what did you like most about what I showed you today?*

When answering this question, they are reselling themselves, telling you the features and benefits they like. You'll be amazed at the success you'll achieve when you get them to dig deeper and deeper. They're likely to realize they do not really have any objections and move forward with the deal.

If they don't sell themselves after step 4—maybe they say they still need to see the value—then you can go back to your notes and respond by presenting them with enough value to overcome that objection.

The first four steps are more important than the response because now they feel heard. Your response to handling the objections will vary quite a bit, depending on the objections, but here are a few key areas that will help you. Whatever the objection is:

1) Go back to past features and benefits that you should have already discussed to explain why the objection should not be a concern.

2) Make sure you constantly tie it back to achieving their desires and goals.

3) Incorporate specific customer stories and examples to show why the objection should not exist. These should be specific stories they can relate to from their concerns, problems they are dealing with, etc.

Mistakes to Avoid

Common Mistake #1: Not digging deep enough for the root objection.

You've got to listen attentively when you ask your prospect to elaborate. If you keep asking them to tell you more (4 or 5 times) to drill down to that singular objection, you'll have a much better understanding of the true issue.

Common Mistake #2: Responding too quickly to handling objections.

Don't jump in too quickly and respond by trying to sell them because you think you know their issue. Remember the analogy of the onion and peeling back the layers? You have to keep clarifying to get to the real objections.

Common Mistake #3: Taking rejection personally.

The reality is that no matter how good you are, you will not close every single deal. You can't take it personally. It may be a matter of timing, external circumstances, and other factors. The important thing is to know that you did do everything that was in your control, and then move on.

Top 10 Rules for Pricing Strategy

Deals can be lost because of how you discuss and present pricing.

Has this ever happened to you or do you have nightmares that it might? You have worked hard to get to the part of the process where the prospect is asking for pricing. You send over the pricing and proposal and wait excitedly to hear back … and it's crickets.

You email to follow up. Call. Text. Send a messenger pigeon. Days and weeks go by. Zero response. Stress sets in and you send desperate emails with discounts. Still no response.

You are afraid you are going to miss your numbers, so you start putting pressure on other opportunities in your pipeline.

Your manager is putting pressure on you because *they* need the sale for their numbers.

There are murmurs of PIPs coming down the pipe. You start second-guessing if you should be in sales and eventually quit because it seems impossible to hit those numbers.

So you go somewhere else and start over. Twelve to eighteen months later, it's the same issue, and the cycle repeats. All because you couldn't get deals to close.

This may be an extreme example for some, but it's not unheard of. Even if you are having marginal success with handling the pricing phase, the following rules can skyrocket your results. If you don't have solid pricing rules to follow, you will lose deals, or you will have stalled deals with a sales cycle that lasts months longer than necessary.

Rule #1: Never present if the prospect is not 100% certain about the solution, you, and your company.

Companies and buyers invest based on their level of certainty in the solution, you, and the company you represent. If they buy purely off price, they'll eventually leave you due to price. If they're uncertain, you missed steps in your process, so go back and uncover what exactly they are uncertain about.

Rule #2: Never present until you are 100% clear on what happens next AFTER the pricing.

If you are unclear about what exactly happens next, your deals will more than likely stall. Ask yourself: "Once the prospect has the pricing, what EXACT steps will they take to decide?"

If you're unclear or it's vague, it's time to slow down to uncover the exact process.

Rule #3: Never present pricing if you don't have executive sponsorship when dealing with a complex organization.

Usually the larger the organization and enterprise opportunity, the more complex the opportunity.

You must uncover who the economic buyer is, a.k.a. the one who releases or shifts the funds.

Their executive sponsorship helps move deals forward and to a close.

Rule #4: Never sell on price, only on value, or else they'll leave you for someone cheaper. Then it's a race to the bottom.

Selling purely on price holds you back from developing the core skills of becoming a great salesperson and leader. Being the cheapest is not sustainable long term.

Rule #5: Keep it wildly simple. No hidden fees or surprises. Be radically transparent. It builds trust. No one likes to be surprised by fees.

Salespeople already get a bad name because we are portrayed in the media as unethical people who do whatever it takes to close the deal. Don't feed into the stereotype, and be wildly transparent about how much it will actually cost.

Rule #6: Present pricing live. Do not send the pricing to a prospect in an email.

Presenting the proposal live either on a Zoom call or a phone call allows you to hear the response so you can get real-time feedback. You can hear what's on their mind, how they are feeling, what they are thinking, and their tonality. You can gather their immediate impact from their body language and tone. Then you can help neutralize if necessary.

This allows you to re-discuss the value your solution brings and helps give them perspective in terms of pricing as a comparison to value. If you don't do this, they could easily misunderstand what they read or even worse, forget all the value you discussed earlier.

It's not about hard closing them on this call, it's about seeing and understanding where they are coming from.

Rule #7: Provide context to ensure they understand all costs.

Here is an example:

> "Ok, Ms. Prospect, let me make sure I'm on the same page as you, alright?
>
> So you currently have your admin manually track hours using Google Sheets, which takes about 10 hours/week to ensure it's inputted properly.

$$10 \text{ hours/week} \times \$15/\text{hour} = \$150/\text{week}$$

$$\$150/\text{week} \times 52 \text{ weeks} = \$7800/\text{year}$$

> So it costs you currently $7800/year just to keep doing what you are doing, is that right?
>
> And that does not include the 10% error rates that are already occurring as you told me, right?
>
> Or when they are out sick so YOU or someone else will have to do it.
>
> Which means that will ultimately drive your cost up because I'm sure your hourly rate is a lot higher too.
>
> So that's 520 hours in the year your admin could be doing something else that would actually help you generate revenue instead of COSTING you.

Our XYZ HR software leads the industry by being 99.99% accurate, is 100% automated, never gets sick, and removes all manual work. Plus, your admin gets back 520 hours to help you generate more money.

With our platinum white glove program, all set-up fees are included, it's just $625/month—$7500 for the year.

So you can see that since we did a thorough and P.O.W.E.R.F.U.L. discovery, we have hard costs and soft costs of what they are currently doing. In comparison to the cost of the solution, there is a crazy amount of value and it's a no-brainer.

Rule #8: If you don't feel good about your pricing, neither will your prospect. You must believe in your pricing.

If you are scared about your pricing, it either means you missed steps in the process and you can tell they haven't bought in, or you do not believe in the solution or company you are selling. If you don't see the value in it, you must ask yourself, what am I doing selling for this company?

Ask yourself: if I was that decision-maker, would I truly invest in this product or solution? You sell how you buy. Cheap people attract cheap buyers and they expect it because that's how they buy.

You must believe in the pricing and your level of conviction must reflect your belief.

Rule #9: Never negotiate via email.

Get them on the phone and have a conversation to come to a close.

Rule #10: Run a refined sales process, uncovering the P.O.W.E.R.F.U.L. elements in discovery.

This is *the* best way to win these opportunities. If you do the upfront process properly, you will have systematically eliminated all of their objections before the pricing conversation.

Asking for Referrals

ALWAYS **ask** for referrals! Why? It's a warm lead, right? That makes it an easier appointment to book. And if this lead knows you are working with people they know in the same business community, it leads to a higher closing ratio.

When you get really good at getting referrals, it relieves a lot of the pressure that comes with prospecting.

Follow this simple three-step process, whether you close the prospect or not:

1. Ask

2. Give direction

3. Incentivize

When you are ending the meeting, here is an example of the conversation:

> *Mr. Prospect, thank you so much for your time today and for your business. I really enjoyed meeting with such a successful executive like yourself. Who else do you know like you that may like a program similar to the one we discussed today?*

Next, you want to give them some **direction** about who you might be looking for. Choose people they can align with easily who might be your target market. Ask them:

- Who are your neighbors?

- Who are your top customers?

- Who are your favorite vendors?

Ask each question one at a time and PAUSE. Wait for them to answer.

Be sure you have something lined up that you can offer as a high-value **incentive** to help you get referrals.

Example:

> *Most people give me 10 referrals, but if you give me 5 today, I'll give you [incentive].*

I used this referral process, and I easily got 7 to 10 referrals every week. And I'm telling you right now, they are super easy to book. So take the above framework, and adjust the language so it fits your style and how you talk.

Remember, even if you don't close the deal, once you have earned the right to ask for the business, you have also earned the right to ask for referrals.

Future Sales Calls

What to do if you don't close on the spot or if it's a multi-call close? There are many situations where this is the case:

- You might not have had a chance to present.

- The prospect realizes that because of the scope of the product or service, they have to bring in another decision-maker.

- You're working a major opportunity that's a sizable deal.

You might not be able to close on the spot and that's ok. However, think of the sales process as an American football game. Every time you engage with the prospect, you want to move the ball as far down the field as fast as you can to score the winning touchdown. This is especially the way you want to think about large enterprise opportunities. Every touchpoint must have the goal of moving the ball down the field as fast as possible.

When I was a rookie with my last company, I went to the annual sales meeting after I had only been with the company for about 14 weeks. One sales leader from a different team came up to me and we started talking.

She asked how my training was going, and I shared with her that I had sold about $500K in total contracted revenue since I started. Most reps would maybe sell $100K-$120K in that timeframe if they were lucky. So I did about 5X the average, and she was blown away.

She asked if I had closed some major accounts, and I said no I had not. She was so confused because she said it's usually a longer sales cycle to close, so how was I doing it?

I didn't really comprehend her questions at the time. I didn't think every sales process had to take some arbitrarily long amount of time. I simply controlled the process upfront. I share this story with you because this leader had been with that company for about six or seven years. She was very successful but she believed the sales cycle should be longer, and I showed her—with less experience—that it didn't have to be that way.

So now you can learn how to do this as well.

Progressing the Sale Forward with 3 Simple Steps

1. Isolate the specific objection (from the H.E.A.R.T. process).

2. Get their agreement about moving forward once you address that objection.

3. Set a date for the next meeting.

Once you're crystal clear about what the root objection is, you'll be able to ask:

> *So if [objection] is addressed, then you feel comfortable moving forward, is that correct?*

> *Aside from [objection], you will move forward, is that right?*

Wait for an affirmative response (get their agreement). Then clarify:

> *If we do [solution], you'd feel comfortable moving forward, is that correct?*

Whatever they need to address, that's where you insert the objection. And then aside from that objection, they will move forward. Get their agreement. Notice that you are clarifying twice.

Tell them that you will get them whatever they need and ask them to give you anything that you might need from them such as numbers or specs. Then set a date for the next meeting.

Get firm next steps for action items with a clear expectation from both parties. This is critical.

> *Ok, since [objection] is your concern, I will do _____ by [specific date] and you will do _____ by [specific date]. Then we will meet on [specific date] to review together. If it all sounds good, we will move forward with paperwork that day, sound good?*

Once you have the meeting, start with a firm agenda each time. Your goal is to review anything that needs to be talked about, answer any questions, and guide the process to a close or to the next step. Rinse and repeat until it's closed. By following this process, you can shorten your normal sales process timeframe.

I like to use the acronym K.I.S.S. and make it positive—Keep It Simple, Superhero.

After the first meeting, email the prospect a recap summarizing everything that is going to happen in the next meeting that you both agreed to. That will *really* impress them.

Common Rookie Mistakes to Avoid

Mistake #1: Not setting FIRM expectations with the prospect for the next steps

Make sure you set firm expectations for the next steps. Don't let them say they will think about it and get back to you or call you next week. That's not a next step, right? That gives them a chance to ghost you when you try to call back.

Mistake #2: Not knowing where you stand with the prospect before you leave

It's really hard to keep moving the ball down the field if you don't know where you stand. Do they like you, do they want to buy from you, do they like your program?

Mistake #3: Being a sales ambassador

Avoid those see-more requests: Can I see more of this or that? Can I see a proposal for this and this? Can you bring me a sample of this and this? ... You don't want to be a sales ambassador, going back and forth, which is why asking those tough questions upfront is so vital. You don't want to waste your time, and you want to shorten your sales cycle. Your goal is not to make them feel good but to solve their problem.

How to Handle Closing a Secondary Decision-Maker

Ideally, you want to meet with the person who can sign the deal and move it forward. For the times when you aren't able to meet with the primary decision-maker, this is the process to follow. Note that this process only works if you have earned their trust and they like you.

Ground rules:

- Clarify, clarify, clarify the decision-making process early and often.

- Know the goals, desires, and benefits desired of EVERY buying influence.

- Trial close early and often.

- Be persistent.

The process:

- Be sure they buy in on what they like.

- Coach them on what to do if the ultimate decision-maker says "no."

- Ask for the business and set the closing call.

Let's say you are at the end of your presentation. You have tried to close them and they say, "We like your solution, but I can't sign today. I need to run this by [insert decision-maker here], and then we should be clear to move."

This is when you would move into this process.

Step #1: "Hey Ms. Prospect, if it was up to you, would you move forward with the program today?"

If they say no, that means you didn't get enough of their goals, generate enough pain, and/or sell enough value. Chances are high you missed one or more steps in the P.O.W.E.R.F.U.L. framework or did not do it effectively. You probably didn't earn the right to ask for the business. You'll want to start diving into exactly what their concerns are. Seek to understand and then make sure you overcome their objections before moving forward in the process or else the deal will more than likely not progress forward.

If they say yes, continue.

Step #2: "Great! What do you like most about the program?"

They tell you what they like.

Step #3: "Great! What else?"

I know this can get awkward but keep asking. At this point, you aren't selling, they are selling themselves. They're saying, "I like this and this and this ..."

Step #4: Then you want to recap.

> *So if I understand you, you like [benefit A] and [benefit B] and [benefit C] about the program because it helps you achieve your goals and desires, is that right?*

Ok, now this is where it may get uncomfortable, but remember: You are not paid to make friends. You are paid to solve problems. You must serve them at the highest level and to help solve their problems. So you want to find out if it was a false objection they gave you when they said they needed to run it by other people, or whether it is a real objection. So ask for the business again by saying this:

> *Perfect. It's clear you NEED this program. Should we go ahead and just get you started?*

You will be surprised how often this works! If they really were honest and they do have to check with another decision-maker, then go on to the next step.

Step #5: "Hey great. What happens if you present this to [decision-maker] and they say no to the program, what are you going to do?"

If they say they will accept the "no," you did not sell enough value! You would then need to uncover what their objections are as it's clear there is still something on their mind that is giving them pause. But if they say they will fight for it and find a way to make it happen, you go on to step #6.

Step #6: "Great! What exactly are you going to say to the decision-maker?"

This is where they may get uncomfortable, but you need to see how they are going to pitch and present your solution. Remember: They are NOT a professional salesperson AND they do not work for your company. They are not going to be able to explain it as well as you, so this is a trial run for them.

If they are weak at handling objections, coach them and have them repeat back what you just said to them. Have them write it down as well. After you feel that they can adequately sell for you, go to step #7.

Step #7: "I want to help you win and accomplish your goals and desires. When are you going to get a chance to discuss this with the decision-maker?"

Find out that info and then plan out clear next steps to take care of the agreement and onboarding. Make sure to have clear deadlines and calendar invites as well.

With this whole process, as with everything, make sure to watch your tonality and read your prospect.

It's amazing how often deals will get closed with this simple process. I find that a lot of the time when they get the pressure to close, they suddenly create some false objection so they don't have to make a decision right then.

These steps help to uncover the real objection so you can handle it properly. More often than not you can close it, or worst-case scenario, your prospect will have the tools to help you sell effectively.

After You Close the Deal

Congratulations! Success—your prospect signed the digital agreement and the deal is closed. Yes, it's time to celebrate, but also be sure that you follow up to be certain that everything gets processed correctly.

Make sure that there isn't a lag in processing any paperwork. Follow up with all necessary departments to ensure customer success. Remember that this is your brand on the table, so you need to ensure that the customer is completely satisfied.

The best way to grow the account is by having a customer who is a superfan of you and your company. Have a built-in cadence to constantly add value to your new customer. If you are handing it off to an account manager or to someone else, the same mindset applies: Make a customer for life.

SECTION EIGHT

90 Days to $500K Blueprint

Knowledge means nothing without action.
Action is what creates results.

When an average rep starts a new job, they may not get much real training or direction. So they end up spending their first one to three months not knowing what to do and not making commissions.

During this initial phase, they are waiting for direction. They may work on their product knowledge and shadow some seasoned reps, but they're still treading water.

Fast forward through those first 90 days and the honeymoon is over. Anxiety sets in as they look at their small or nonexistent pipeline and their small or nonexistent paycheck. And thus starts the rollercoaster ride with all its ups and downs and twists and turns.

I have come up with a strategy that's designed to move you rapidly through growth, learning, and pipeline within the first 90 days. More importantly, it will set up the foundation for you for the future, so you can avoid the crazy rollercoaster ride.

Even if you have been in your role for a while, but are struggling with it, you can use this same basic process. It works with both experienced and rookie teams. It works whether you're in a completely brand new, full-cycle sales role, at a new company, or in a new industry with zero pipeline.

I've executed it with an underperforming team and closed $500K+ in TCV (total contract value) in 90 days and generated over $2M in qualified pipeline. That's 4–5X the average of a new rep. As I continued to compound my results, I got promoted. Less than nine months later, I helped to turn the entire sales team around.

This blueprint is very simple, but don't mistake the simplicity for lack of effectiveness. I am going to break this down into segments so you can jump right in and apply them immediately.

Days 1–5: Belief and Foundational Frameworks

BELIEF AND FOUNDATIONAL FRAMEWORKS

STEP 1	STEP 2	STEP 3	STEP 4	STEP 5

Build belief and understand the ICP inside and out.	Build department connections.	Hang out with the reps who are winning.	Build a routine.	Build a list and do your research.

One of the biggest challenges when starting with a new company is selling to potential clients that your product or service is the best. You need massive belief and conviction in what you're selling. So that's why Step 1 deals with building belief and understanding your customer.

Step 1: Build belief and understand the ICP inside and out.

Get into the head of your ICP. Learn their copy, messaging, who the ideal customer is, why they buy, core benefits, etc. Look at case studies and review customer interviews.

Then you want to start writing out the copy messaging for emails and phone frameworks.

When I started out, I contacted current customers and asked them a myriad of questions to glean as much info as I could to understand their motives and what was driving their buyer decisions:

- What do they like about the products? What don't they like?

- What are the benefits?

- What competitors did they use in the past?

- Why did they switch to our company?

- How do they use our products and services?

Step 2: Build department connections.

Be sure you have a strong support system. You want to map out the entire sales process from end to end so that you understand the full process from cold prospecting to onboarding and customer success. Understand WHY it's done that way and the impact you might have if you deviate or shift from this process.

This is wildly important because these are also people that can help you to instill belief in yourself.

For example, if you don't feel comfortable with a customer getting onboarded, it will be hard for you to have the level of conviction you must have to make sales.

I literally went to every department head and had a conversation to cover most of the mistakes reps might make and what I needed to do to avoid them. They were happy to tell me all the mistakes that sales reps had made. I learned so much and became a better business professional.

Step 3: Hang out with the reps who are winning.

What are they doing consistently and successfully? Listen to conversations they are having with customers and find out what the most common objections are and how they handle them.

Take notes on the questions they are asking. What are they looking for in their discovery calls? What is the order they are following? Map this out in detail as a framework.

Then start practicing the scripts and frameworks for mastery so it feels buttery smooth. Practice, practice, practice! This is what athletes do to be the best. They spend 99% of their time practicing and only 1% competing on the field. Remember these are foundations you are building, so the base needs to be firm before you move on to the next step.

Step 4: Build a routine.

Write out clear, tangible outcomes from start to finish for each work day. Map it out and have it focus heavily on income-producing activities that will add to the pipeline, move the pipeline, or close deals within the pipeline.

Step 5: Build a list and do your research.

Include the following:

- Low hanging fruit

- Lost opportunities

- Tribal knowledge (maybe someone on the team has mentioned a specific company that past reps have tried to close or work on, but it isn't listed in the CRM)

- Current customers, new departments (a.k.a. what's closest to the money)

When I got to this step, I literally went through all the activity in the CRM from the past 90 days and added those to my list.

I looked at all the lost opportunities and did the same thing.

We weren't allowed to sell to current customers so I couldn't use that one, but we had some national accounts with a local presence, so I made a list of those. Once I was done, I had a list of 200–300 people that I could start working off of the following week.

Outcomes from Days 1-5

- Create massive belief in the desired results of the solution you are planning to sell, as well as in your company and in the support systems in place for success. If you lack conviction in your foundation, it doesn't matter how good your sales process is, you will not have consistent success.

- Clearly defined ICP and psychographics—you understand what their true buying motivations are beyond surface-level benefits.

- You have built a list you feel confident in and frameworks mapped out for the phones/emails.

- You have practiced and role-played hundreds of times so you are mentally ready for next week.

- You have a framework down for the process.

Days 6–10: Sales Process Testing

Step 1: Set a tangible goal to go after.

This goal should be output-based versus outcome-based because there is still so much you don't know. An output-based example would be that you make 100 calls. Setting a goal of closing two deals would be outcome-based.

Step 2: Run the routine tight and start outbound ASAP.

You should have time blocks for your entire day to dictate when you make calls, send emails, etc.

Step 3: Make note of all the objections on the phone, email, etc.

Uncover any objections, and write down industry lingo you don't know. Get someone you trust to help you to understand it.

Step 4: If you make any discovery calls this week, run the calls.

Remember that your "rookie energy" is high, so take advantage of this. The more repetitions you can focus on, the faster you will learn.

Step 5: Keep a daily log of your metrics.

The more you build your self-awareness, the faster you will learn, so keep a daily log of your metrics. This includes your open rates, reply rates, number of calls you make, number of decision-makers you talk to, gatekeeper conversion ratio, etc. You want to track EVERY part of the funnel so you can keep improving it.

Write down 5 key learnings every day and how you will apply what you have learned. The key is to look for common themes so you can create a tight feedback loop that will help you to increase your self-awareness.

Many people make the mistake of not doing this part, and as a result, they don't improve because they don't have the awareness.

Step 6: By the end of the week, you want to start understanding what is converting well and what isn't.

Make note of what's working well, and tweak the parts that aren't.

Step 7: Keep practicing in your free time.

Practice your full end-to-end sales process, and incorporate the toughest objections you've learned.

I was in full cycle sales, so we did everything from knocking on doors to emails to LinkedIn. I like to be in front of people face to face so I can read their facial expressions and see their body language. I went out and knocked on the doors of over 300 businesses in my first week alone.

My number one goal was not to close, but to *learn*. I wanted to know what objections people were using and what competitors they might be using. I wanted to walk into these businesses that were not my target so that I could use them to practice.

I remember I actually booked 16–20 appointments by walking into those businesses. Was I exhausted? Absolutely! Could I do this every week? No way. But I learned so much valuable information by applying the basic frameworks I built out in days 1–5.

Outcomes from Days 6–10:

- Your output should be at least 2X (minimum) that of the average rep, as your goal is accelerated learning.

- You understand at a deeper level the most common objections and desires of your ICP.

- You are now also loading prospects into your pipeline. Even if you have a low conversion for each step in the sales process, you should be adding and growing a qualified pipeline.

Days 11–30: Refinement

You will be rinsing and repeating much of what you did in days 6–10, but now your key is execution by refinement.

- Your output needs to stay, at a minimum, 2X the average rep, but you will focus on improving conversions at every stage.

    o An example of this would be if you have a 20% open rate, you want to test so that you can shift it to 30%+. If 50% convert from discovery to demo, then drive toward reaching 75%.

- Do the following to boost self-awareness:

    1. Continue to track daily metrics, logging 5 daily learnings and how you will apply them.

    2. Listen to all your recordings and take notes on how to improve. If you are unsure, ask for feedback from someone who is consistently crushing it. You need unbiased feedback. Nothing changes if you don't change!

    3. Use this feedback and track your progress.

    4. Continue to practice for mastery in your off-time.

Outcomes from Days 11–30:

- Depending on the deal size and complexity, you may be close to closing some deals or have deals that have moved much further in the pipeline.

- If it's a transactional sales process, you should have closed opportunities at this point.

- Your pipeline should be juiced up as well with qualified opportunities.

- Each conversion point in your sales process should be progressing forward.

- At this point, if your results are not better than the average rep, that's a huge red flag! It means that there are gaps in your sales process, and they can show up anywhere from targeting, copy, and messaging, to how you run your sales call or your sales skills development. Locate and fix your weak spots immediately.

Days 31–90: Preparing for Scale

• If you are progressing nicely, continue to tighten down your sales process with refinements while maintaining a 2X+ output.

   Take advantage of your rookie energy! You will eventually get too busy to practice at this level, so take the time now and it will pay you dividends down the road.

• Continue to focus on self-awareness and improvements.

   1. The mistake that many people make is, if they have some progress and success, they stop doing the work that got them there. They stop reflecting and building self-awareness, they stop tracking their metrics and looking at their numbers, they stop listening to recordings of their sales calls. Fast forward six months later, they are struggling and they can't figure out why.

   2. Eliminate objections proactively and start testing them in your sales process.

• Continue to run the routine tight and continue to juice the funnel.

- The lists you build to work off should now be segmented into deal sizes that will drive toward helping you achieve your personal goals. Be strategic.

This is what I did. Based off my comp plan, I made sure I followed a 70/20/10 rule. To break that down:

- 70% of the deals fell into a total-contract-value-bucket size which I designated as greater than $20K but less than $80K,

- 20% fell into a different bucket size of $80K–$120K, and

- 10% were beyond the $150K TCV bucket.

This would reflect across the board, from the list I was building to the opportunities that I was running, to the deals I was closing. So instead of putting an arbitrary list of prospects to call on that vary in size, this allows you to be strategic. You ensure a diverse pipeline of prospects and deal sizes, which also spreads out the risk you have in sales cycle lengths.

Outcomes from Days 31–90:

- Deals should be progressing through the sales cycle efficiently.

- Deals should be closing.

- Your pipeline should be at minimum 2–4X everyone else's if you have been consistent.

- You have a repeatable and scalable process from outbound to close.

- Your confidence should be very high, as each week you should be compounding your skills and pipeline.

- If you aren't seeing these results, you've missed some steps.

Troubleshooting Questions for Not Hitting $500K in 90 Days

If you've been executing the 90-day plan but you're not seeing the results you want to achieve, ask yourself the following questions:

- Did you execute the plan EXACTLY as I have laid it out?

- Where is the constraint in your sales process? Is it in the top, middle, or end of the funnel?

- Assuming you have product market fit, are you as skilled at each stage of the sales process as you believe you are? If you have been tracking your data, your numbers will tell the story. Numbers don't lie.

I was talking to a rep who told me they had a great closing ratio. They said they closed at around 80% but they weren't hitting their numbers.

I started diving into it. It was true that they were booking a lot of meetings, but the bookings weren't qualified and they were counting that ratio from proposal to close instead of from booking to close.

Because they were not calculating the ratios using the correct data, they didn't realize that their true closing ratio was closer to 10%. Once we had the data, we could work on better targeting, improving the discovery, and having better control over the sales process.

This is why it is key to put your ego aside and be transparent. Here are some questions to ask yourself:

- Are you effective at multi-channel outbound?

- Are you effective in running discovery calls?

- Are you effective in navigating a complex opportunity and guiding it to a close?

- Are you effective at presenting/demoing?

- Are you effective at follow-up?

- Are you effective at closing?

- Are you effective at showing up consistently as a person of value to the ultimate decision-makers (are you a rep or a pro)?

Remember, reps don't close a lot of business, pros do. Your numbers tell you an objective story. If you are still struggling, get help from someone who has been wildly successful consistently.

SECTION NINE

The Basics of Selling 6- and 7-Figure+ Enterprise Deals

_____

You'll be paid in direct proportion to the value you create in the marketplace.

—T. Harv Eker

I looked at my phone. Finally! The person I'd been waiting anxiously to hear from—the VP of Operations. I had been trying to reach him for about two weeks to get the final ok to close a huge deal I had been working on. He had given me a verbal heads-up, but I needed to get the final go-ahead so we could get the paperwork signed.

It was a large deal for me of about $240K/year with a total contract value of over $1 million, so it was going to cover a large portion of my quota.

I had been getting more and more nervous as I tried to reach my prospect without any success via the phone, emails, and mutual contacts.

As soon as I heard his voice, I knew something was wrong.

"Hey Marcus, I'm really sorry but we ended up going with someone else. The CFO decided to go with a different vendor that he has had a long-term relationship with."

I felt like I had been punched in the gut! He had given me the verbal that they were going to move forward with us, so I thought it was a done deal. I had already told my boss it was pretty much closed, and he was counting on this hitting for the quarter to make up for the rest of the underperforming team's quota deficit. I was not looking forward to that conversation as I could already picture his face getting red with anger.

Even worse, this account alone would have earned me a high 5-figures in commission, and I had mentally planned on using the money to surprise my new wife by taking her on a romantic vacation somewhere exotic. I had already told her about the plan and she was excited. My heart sank just thinking about disappointing her.

After I got over the shock and disappointment, I reflected back and realized that I had missed parts of my whole sales process: from not doing effective discovery to not multithreading (involving multiple different buying influences or stakeholders at a company to move a deal toward a close) properly to not doing a deep dive into all the buying influences.

It was a big wake-up call. There were a lot of mistakes over time that forced me to analyze my whole sales process. I started to figure out what was missing. Then, I determined what I could have done differently—in advance—to increase my closing ratio.

Realizing how many opportunities I had ALREADY lost in the past due to these simple mistakes, I could see that those invisible gaps had easily cost me hundreds of thousands of dollars in commissions. Then it hit me like a ton of bricks: If I didn't improve my sales skills to the next level, the opportunity cost of lost future deals would easily be worth millions of dollars more.

And that did not even include the opportunity cost and impact of what I could do with the commissions by investing that money! Not to mention the future promotional opportunities and the indomitable confidence that would come from being able to handle and close multiple 7- to 8-figure opportunities.

Another major realization I had was that running every sales process hyper efficiently would increase my throughput and win rate across the board. It's about controlling what I can control and ensuring every single touchpoint counts like an 8-figure deal, no matter the company size. Smaller deals can become bigger maxed-out ones, and that has helped me to close 6-, 7-, and 8-figure deals significantly faster.

I have continually refined this over time and continue to refine, and I have taught other reps and my students how to close deals in 2–4 months that might have taken 12–18 months to close. I want to share those pieces with you in this section so that you can learn this process.

Remember: the basics I'm going to share here are a big part of it, but also having the readiness to use all the techniques of the sales process that I have shared with you so far in this book is key as well.

Why do you want to close large enterprise accounts?

- They are great for your bank account!

- They allow you to achieve your quota more quickly.

- They are great for credibility.

- The more complex the deal, the more fun it is.

Getting large accounts in your pipeline doesn't happen overnight. It takes time to get them into your funnel. But there are mistakes I see professionals make that you want to avoid. Each of these seven mistakes is self-explanatory, but you would be shocked to know how many salespeople I see make them every day.

Seven Common Mistakes to Avoid

1. No process in place to prospect or work it consistently

2. Lack of follow-up or follow-thru

3. Lack of strategy while working the account

4. Treating the large accounts like small accounts

5. Not effectively managing all buying influences

6. Not having a diverse account size pipeline

7. Overcomplicating the process

Navigating the Sales Cycle and Process

With large accounts, the overall elements of the sales process will stay the same, but you will have more stakeholders to navigate and work through, more meetings, more emails, and more calls.

This means that you need to stay organized, control what you can control, and navigate all buying influences to a close.

I want to be sure you have a good understanding of all the buying influences, or stakeholders. I learned these from Robert Miller and Stephen Heiman's book *Strategic Selling,* and it's helped me close a lot of big deals. There are four types of buying influences:

- Economic buyer

- Technical buyer

- User buyer

- Coach

We discussed personality types already, but this is about their actual role in the company, and what they do.

Economic Buyer: This is the only player who can truly say yes, even if others say no. It's not always based on their title in the company. If there is a board of directors, there is always one person with more sway.

Let's say you are working a complex deal. They have a budget of $50K to spend on software. All of the buying influences are telling you "yes," but if the economic buyer says "no," they can take those funds and use them toward something else like a new HVAC system. They hold the ultimate power; they are the true final decision-maker.

In a perfect world, you would only meet with economic buyers, but this isn't going to be the case because deal cycles get more complex. However, do your best to start opportunities from the top down even if they are 99% removed from the solution you sell. When you can get executive sponsorship from the economic buyer to begin with, it becomes much easier to work the relationships with every buying influence below them.

Also, similar to what we've discussed before, every buying decision needs to be tied to the overall initiatives of an organization, so when you are speaking to the C-suite, you can hear it directly from them. Then you can bridge the gap between your solution and the problem it solves, and then tie it to achieving company objectives.

Technical Buyer: This buyer can't say yes to you, as far as signing the paperwork and moving forward, but they *can* say no. In large enterprise deals, these are usually the people who are searching for vendors. If you are meeting with someone and they say, "I can make decisions, I just need to check with (decision-maker)," chances are they are a technical buyer. They usually have a set of requirements, and they love to act like they are the final decision-maker—even though they're not.

User Buyer: These buyers are using the products or services and are the ones directly impacted by them. If there is already a vendor in place, these are the buyers who know all the pros and cons and what's really going on.

The rookie mistake many reps make is that they start their sales process here. The issue is that it's much harder to sell up the chain versus down the chain. Although you will need to involve them at one point in the sales process, I find it's better to meet with them after getting executive sponsorship from the economic buyer.

Coach: These buyers want you to win. They are huge fans. They tell you all the details to ensure your position to win. They will "coach" you and help you navigate through the process.

The hardest part as a sales professional in these deals is navigating the complex process and moving the players like chess pieces in order to close the deal.

There could be multiple technical buyers and user buyers, so you need to know ALL the players. Make sure you stay properly organized using your CRM or other tools to ensure you map out each major account and don't miss any buying influences.

It's not easy to close deals, but they are worth it. At the end of the day, even though the deal complexity is much higher, it's important to keep things simple. An enterprise opportunity is simply a business that has a big problem, and your job is to figure out how to solve it with the stakeholders involved.

If you run an efficient sales process, like the one you've read so far, you'll be able to close big and small deals much faster than the competition.

Key Takeaways

Ground Rules:

- You sell who you see. You have to build in time weekly to prospect for new large accounts and to work existing ones. Hedge your bets properly and have a diverse pipeline.

- Be proactive and be creative.

- Break it down into simple goals. If you have a 20% closing ratio and you want to close six enterprise deals a year, then you need to have a minimum of 30 enterprise accounts in your pipeline at all times. Make the math work!

- You must have a good value proposition or solution.

- The fortune is in the follow-up, so be sure you nurture all buying influences consistently, bringing value to every single touchpoint and always moving the ball forward.

- Be consistent with your prospecting and your process.

- Stay hyper-organized using your CRM to map each enterprise account out so you don't drop the ball on them.

- Play the long game. It's a marathon, not a sprint. You don't want the process to take forever, but you also don't want to rush through the process.

- Every touchpoint must always bring value.

SECTION TEN

Develop a Bulletproof Sales Mindset

If you work hard at your job you can make a living. If you work hard on yourself, you will make a fortune.

—Jim Rohn

Tested and Proven Success Strategies

In 2017, I was leading a large sales organization with 110+ employees. I had just finished a record-breaking year, so in 2018, my market quota was increased by 15%. That may not seem like a lot, but when you have a nine-figure quota, it's a massive increase!

On top of that, there were issues going on with some of the managers—a manager had made a bad decision, and HR wanted to make sure I wasn't involved. Also, a young manager passed away due to alcoholism. We also had all sorts of personnel issues due to a prior $2.2 billion acquisition.

On the personal side, I was going nuts. I was traveling almost every week while we had a young kid at home, and my parents, who had been married for over 40 years, were fighting like crazy and talking about divorce.

I was mentally, emotionally, spiritually, and physically drained. Many times during that year, I thought about quitting and finding a job with less stress. But because of the mindset I had developed and continue to develop, we ended up finishing 2018 by breaking even more records and sending more people to President's Club because of our efforts.

I'm not sharing this story to brag, but to give you an example where I would not have been able to accomplish what I did if it weren't for the strategies I'm going to reveal in this chapter.

Your Best Competitive Advantage

Anyone successful in life, whether they are a great minister, leader, dentist, parent, or salesperson, has some core principles that they live by. Some are hopefully a given if you are reading this book: ethics, honesty, integrity, etc. These are expected if you're a pro.

If you want the results that come from a bulletproof sales mindset, you've got to work at it. And once you achieve it, you've got to keep working at it.

Developing a bulletproof mindset gives you a competitive advantage that boosts your confidence like nothing else.

Everything you do affects your confidence. Either your actions will add to your confidence, subtract, multiply, or divide. It's basic math.

If you want bulletproof confidence, look first at your actions.

- What are your actions telling you?

- Where are they leading you?

- Are they adding to your confidence or subtracting from it?

When you get strong results, you develop a strong mindset. As you build up a bulletproof sales mindset, you'll get bulletproof sales results.

It's a cycle that can either serve you or hurt you.

- Your mindset impacts your beliefs.

- Your beliefs impact your actions.

- Your actions impact your results.

- Your results impact your confidence.

- Your confidence impacts your mindset.

BULLETPROOF SALES MINDSET

Remember, every decision you make will either add to or subtract from your confidence. And confidence is the key to winning in sales.

All of the core principles that I am going to reveal have been tested and proven by me, as well as by all the people I've trained over the last decade. If you don't want to be average, don't do what average people do. Dare to do it differently.

Core Principle #1: Everything you want lies outside of your comfort zone.

If you want to achieve something you've never achieved before, you must be willing to do things you've never done before. Some of the things that you've learned so far may make you uncomfortable because you haven't done them before. But they are very effective—if you put in the work. Doing something once and expecting that you'll be perfect at it with incredible results is the wrong expectation. That's like doing one workout, realizing you're still not in the shape you want to be in, and then concluding that "working out doesn't work." It makes zero sense.

Success is not comfortable or easy. If it was EASY, then *every* salesperson would be earning millions of dollars and crushing it. Lean toward discomfort and get comfortable with the uncomfortable, and you'll stand out among the crowd.

Core Principle #2: Focus is a superpower.

Warren Buffett says, "If there's one skill that I wish everyone could have that I really attribute to my success, it's focus."

To gain mastery over a skill, narrow your focus. Don't multi-task! Don't read 10 books at once, read one book and master it.

Don't buy 30 sales courses, buy one and master it.

If you want to be massively successful, you have to narrow your focus and eliminate distractions. If you are writing a business email, don't be checking social media at the same time or reading the texts on your phone.

Being intentional creates results. When you follow this principle, you will see better results.

Core Principle #3: Destroy A.N.T.s

Have you ever had ants running around in your house? They find a way in, and they multiply. Even though they are very small, they can be very destructive. In mindset terminology, A.N.T. stands for Automatic Negative Thoughts. These are the daily negative thoughts that run wild through your brain creating chaos and doubt. It's essentially death by a thousand paper cuts.

These daily negative thoughts add up over time and eat away at your confidence. Once that first A.N.T. starts running around in your brain, others quickly follow, and soon you'll go from one unsuccessful cold call to "I will never be able to do this."

The more ants that crawl into your head, the more they will destroy you. Once they take hold, it may cause you to lose your productivity for that day or that week, or maybe even longer!

You need to develop routines to destroy these ants, which I will discuss in a later chapter.

Core Principle #4: If you work hard at your job, you will make a living. If you work hard on yourself, you will make a fortune.

Warren Buffet has said, "The best investment you can make is in yourself. The more you learn, the more you earn." This is coming from one of the richest men in the world.

I've found this to be wildly true because when you master high leverage skills like sales, communication, influence, and copywriting, they pay dividends every single year.

Elite salespeople know this and that's why they invest in themselves with coaches, programs, and mentors even before they get good. Then once they are great, they continue to invest to stack on more skills. Think of elite sports athletes like Lebron James. He is known for investing over $1M/year in himself as that is what helps him to make the most money and get the greatest return.

Because you are reading this book, I know you are invested in becoming part of the top 1%. You are investing in yourself to take your game to the next level.

Core Principle #5: When you get rejected, lose a deal, or are in a "sales slump," ask yourself ...

1. What can I learn from this?

2. How can I apply this to benefit my future?

3. What can be great about this?

4. What can I do to prevent this from happening again?

5. What can I do today that my future self will thank me for?

Posing these questions puts you in a problem-solving mentality. This is important because no matter how good you are at the game, no matter how well you master the sales process, stuff still happens. You will get rejected. You will lose a deal.

Life is about the things that happen to us both personally and professionally. Being alive means having issues and problems. But remember this: your circumstances do not determine where you go, they only determine where you started from.

When you have a tough day or a rough week, walk yourself through these types of questions so you can learn and be proactive.

Goal Setting

Most people lack clarity and goals, so they never achieve them. They may be afraid to dream big because they don't have the faith that they can accomplish those dreams.

I grew up very poor. My family never made a six-figure income. When I graduated from college at 21, I made up my mind that by the time I reached 30, I was going to make six figures.

My boss Paul was around 45 at the time and made about $60k

a year. It seemed really hard to be able to make six figures, but I believed I could do it.

Fast forward a couple of years, and I achieved my goal fairly quickly. Once I achieved it, I thought to myself, *What the heck? Why did I set such a low goal? What if I had set a higher goal of $1 million? What could I have achieved then?*

My mindset was that if I set my goal at $1 million, even if I fell short and made $300k, I would have been super happy to make that at age 22.

I'm sharing this story because I set my goal too low to start with and it really hurt me. I'm going to share with you what I wish I knew back then to set up proper goals.

MSTW Goal Setting

The method that I have found to be the most simplistic is the MSTW goal-setting method. It stands for measurable, specific, timebound, and why.

Measurable: Your goal has to be able to be measured. For example: I want to achieve a million-dollar net worth.

Specific: Be precise about what that will include, for example, cash, stocks, bonds, real estate, and IRAs.

Timebound: Specify a certain amount of time, such as 12 months.

Why: Knowing your why is really important. It's what will get you out of bed on those days when you just don't feel like it.

So set your goals by asking yourself: What would my goals be if I knew I couldn't fail?

When you are setting goals that involve money, this is what I find that a majority of the top performers do: They make sure that they tie that number back to the number of sales required to achieve it. So take your goal and divide it by your average commission per deal.

So for example, say you want to buy a house and you need a down payment of $50K. Your average commission on a sale is $2,500, so you need 20 sales to make your goal.

$$\$50K \div \$2{,}500 = 20 \text{ sales}$$

$$20 \text{ sales} \div 12 \text{ months} = 1.6 \text{ sales per month}$$

If you want to accomplish this goal in 12 months, you need to close about 1.6 sales per month. Doesn't it sound much easier to navigate making 1.6 sales per month than just saying I need to make $50K? It's much more digestible. (And yes, you can adjust the numbers to offset taxes, to build a buffer, etc., but the principle is the same.)

This method can apply to anything. When you are investing in yourself, your development, and your future, view it in sales numbers.

Once you set these goals, obstacles are going to show up. It's just the way the world works. So you need a consistent way to maintain confidence, which is built off of taking action, which creates results. This is where mindset routines come into play.

Common Mistakes Keeping You from Achieving Your Goals

1. Not owning and believing the core principles. Don't let your ego get in the way and start to think that these principles don't apply to you. The more I learn in life, the more I realize I don't know. So put aside your ego.

2. Not reviewing your GOALS and WHYS consistently. As you start to put your plans into action, you will be able to see success in some areas right away, but others may require more time or some tweaking. It's easy to lose confidence, but you want to stay focused on the bigger picture, so consistently reviewing your goals and whys is important.

3. Your goals are too small. You want to set massive goals, so big that they scare you. What would you go after if you knew you couldn't fail?

4. Not being crystal clear on your why. Know what drives you and know your purpose. You may have to dig deep to uncover your why but it's so important.

Mindset Routines to Start Your Day

It's important to prime your mind for success. I start my day at 5 a.m. I do a physical workout of 360 to 480 repetitions of one specific muscle group. This gets me fired up and physically ready to start my day.

Next, I listen to an audiobook to feed my mind. I go through a series of affirmations that make me feel empowered for five to 10 minutes. Then I do my perfect day visualization. If one year from now, I have achieved all my goals that I set for that year, what would that perfect day look like? From the moment I wake up until I go to sleep that night, what I would be doing, feeling, etc.? I have made a recording of myself verbalizing this perfect day, and I listen to it and visualize it.

In addition, I visualize the upcoming day and exactly how I want it to unfold. Then I review my goals. This routine takes me about an hour and a half to prime my mind.

Since I am starting my day out strong, I want to end my day the same way, so I have an evening mindset routine as well.

Before I go to bed, I write out a gratitude list—three to five things I am grateful for that day. Even if I had a really rough day, I write what I am grateful for. This is so powerful because it helps me stay positive. There is always something I can be grateful for—I had a great dinner, I have a wonderful kid, I learned something new ...

Then I review my goals again. So for five minutes in the morning and five minutes at night, this helps me refocus on where I am going in my one-, three-, and five-year plans.

After that, I read a physical book (staying away from EMF and blue light at night), something nonfiction to feed my mind. I meditate for five to 10 minutes, and then my day is done.

Now, you need to build *your* version of these routines and find what works for *you*. These routines help to give you control in your life because you can control your morning and your evening to prime your mind. You can't always control the external circumstances and other people, but you can control this.

Create your own unique routine that you can stick to consistently to prime your mind.

Top Performer Routine Characteristics

There are many important characteristics to being a top performer, but here are a few key ones:

1. They are consistent in their behaviors.

2. They are honest with themselves.

3. They are productive versus just being "busy."

4. Their weekly routine incorporates the 80/20 rule. 20% of the things they do drive 80% of their results. Thus their week is focused heavily around as much of the 20% of income-producing activities.

5. They know their goals and their numbers. They know their goals inside and out, what they want to accomplish from income, and their quota. They live to exceed and destroy quota!

6. They execute regardless of how they feel.

7. They incorporate what I call the "M5" core health buckets to be considered truly healthy:

- Mind: They do whatever they can to protect their headspace.

- Matter: They are clear on their purpose and execute based on it.

- Marriage: They treat people in their inner circle like partners. (Pro tip: Choose a partner who makes you better. It's an important way to think.)

- Muscle: They work out consistently as part of their core routine.

- Money: They manage their money wisely from an income and wealth-building perspective.

When you have all five of these incorporated, you can have true health because you are tapping into all of the areas of your life.

Mentorship

When we think we know it all, that is when we start going backward. The top salespeople know that there are never-ending opportunities to learn and improve. The more they learn, the more they realize how much they don't know.

There is always someone out there who has gone through the learning curve and is accomplishing goals that you aspire to.

That's why mentorship is a key area in having a bulletproof sales mindset. Having a mentor gives you perspective. You want to choose someone who has already achieved what you want to achieve. The fastest way to learn is always through someone else who has already made the mistakes as they can cut down your learning curve drastically.

When you surround yourself with the right people, they will challenge you to excel and grow. Great mentors help you unleash the greatness inside of you and help you reach milestones you never thought possible. Another great benefit is that they also can support you mentally and emotionally.

In order to achieve what we've never achieved before, we must be willing to do what we've never done before. Having the emotional support of a mentor who believes in you can be the difference in whether or not you believe in yourself.

Personal Health and Wellness

Your body is a high-performance machine, so you need to treat it as one. The way you take care of your body impacts how you feel and how you think.

When you work out regularly and eat healthy food, you look better as well, which tends to add more confidence. Success takes stamina.

In general, I find that the most successful people are in good shape. They are tapping into the M5. Part of peak performance is having a body in peak health.

Maximizing Your Time

As a sales professional, you need to understand that time is your most valuable asset. Maximizing time is critical because you can never get it back. You want to choose how you spend your time wisely because what you focus on is what you achieve. Plan the work and work the plan.

As we talked about in the last section, routine helps you create focused habits. Focused habits lead to results. So you are the results of the habits you have in place, whether they are good or bad.

Know Your Numbers to Build Your Routine

You can't build your financial routine if you don't know your numbers. You can't make a top income consistently if you don't know how to get there. Your routine has to reflect the numbers and goals you want to achieve.

Numbers you need:

- Your annual income goal

- Average commission and bonuses per deal (an easy way to do this is to take the total commission plus bonuses for last year and divide by the number of deals you closed). If you just started, you could ask your sales leader for an estimate. A ballpark is fine as we just need it for direction.

- Your conversion rate (number of closed deals divided by your number of first meetings)
    - Ex. Last year you closed 100 deals and you had 300 first meetings.

      ○   100 ÷ 300 = 0.33 or a 33% conversion rate

- Your compensation plan

Your routine needs to reflect the number of discovery calls you need to run each week or month to achieve your goals. Once you know that number, then you can work toward that for your top-of-the-funnel efforts.

How to calculate it out:

1. Annual income goal = base salary + total in commissions and bonuses (C) + (B) required

$250,000 = $50K + $200K

So you would need to generate $200K in commissions and bonuses

2. Total in C + B ÷ avg. C + B per deal = # of deals needed (let's assume $2K in commissions and bonuses per deal)

$200K ÷ $2K = 100 deals needed

3. # of deals ÷ conversion ratio = # of discovery calls needed

100 ÷ .33 = 303 discovery calls needed

4. # of discovery calls ÷ # of working weeks = # of discovery calls each week

303 ÷ 48 = 6.3 per week

Now that you have your numbers, you need to build your routine so that you can accomplish these goals. These are conservative numbers that you can start with. You want to strive for increasing your deal size and getting really good at closing. The key is doing the math so you have targets to work toward on a daily and weekly basis.

Income-Producing Activities (IPAs)

Income-producing activities are the things that you do that are going to make you money! This is where the 80/20 rule comes into play again. When you think about it, 20% of your activities will deliver 80% of your results.

As a sales professional, you have a lot of responsibilities, including:

- Cold calling
- Discovery calls
- Demos/Presentations
- Closing
- Handling objections
- Using a CRM for funnel management
- Creating proposals
- Follow-up phone calls
- Research
- Emails
- Dealing with issues

- Talking through all the decision-makers
- Running samples back and forth

The list goes on and on, right? But at the end of the day, only a few of your daily activities are income-producing:

- Prospecting
- Closing
- Growing accounts/customer success

That's right: adding to your pipeline, moving deals in your pipeline, or closing deals in your pipeline. This is what gets you paid! So your routine must be dialed to maximize this 20% and eliminate as much as you can in the other 80%.

It's easy to find reasons to be busy in nonproductive areas, so remove environments that distract you. For example, if you get a lot of notifications on your phone for different applications, turn them off or delete the app.

How to Create Your Routine

When I was in college, I had all the time in the world. I could do a two-hour workout in the gym whenever I wanted.

Once I graduated and started a job, I had more obligations and my schedule was really busy. But I still made time for my workout, cutting it from two hours to an hour and a half.

Then we had a baby, and suddenly I couldn't justify the time. It was half an hour to the gym, half an hour drive back home, plus the hour and a half actual workout.

I sat down and analyzed what I actually did at the gym and realized how much time I was wasting. I would get to the gym and sit around scrolling through social media for 10–20 minutes. Then I would start going through the machines, but I would take time between machines to look at my phone. And then when I was changing in the locker room, I would scroll through social media again for another 10–15 minutes.

I started to eliminate distractions. I stopped looking at social media. I would change into my workout clothes before I left, so I was ready to jump right in at the gym.

Those were the small things. The big change was the workout itself. I realized that if I came up with a better routine and planned it all out, I could be more efficient.

I mapped out the exact exercise machines and weights that I would do for my entire workout. This way, I could go down the list and hit the routine. If someone was on a machine, I would go on to the next exercise and come back to that one later.

Now I was able to do that hour and a half routine in 30 minutes! I started applying this to other parts of my life as well because I realized how much time I was wasting here and there.

I began running bigger teams at work and traveling more. I literally started mapping out every minute from the moment I woke up to when I went to bed. This way I would only do things that would serve me.

I wasn't perfect, but if I could stick to it 80% of the time, I got much better results. I realized this was similar to the sales routine I had developed where I would only focus on income-producing activities.

So this is what I recommend you do to create your own efficient routine: Start with a list of all the activities you currently do. Next, highlight the 20% that drives 80% of your results. I would guess that it will be similar to what we have discussed.

Now you want to map it into a schedule, incorporating the 20% as much as possible. Incorporate the bulletproof routines we discussed earlier as well.

You also want to incorporate health and wellness and the M5.

Now with all this said, understand that this is a journey. You build the perfect routine and you are all psyched to follow it every day. But that's not life. There will be dips, rocks, and obstacles that come your way. You're going to hit walls, which is normal.

The people who succeed in sales (and in life) understand that it's not only about the resources they have access to, but also how resourceful they are when they hit a wall. Problems are inevitable. The only time you won't run into issues is when you're no longer alive.

So what do you do when you feel unmotivated? What tactical things can you do when you are in a sales slump?

1. First off, go back to the routine: Are you consistent with all the M5 buckets?

2. How long have you been doing the routine? Give it 3–4 weeks before you change it, but if you have been doing it for a while, maybe it's not working for you anymore. It's ok to change it to find one that works.

3. Are you reviewing your big goals? Are you truly motivated by them?

4. Do you have an accountability partner that makes you better?

5. Are you planning your days and weeks ahead of time? You want to have appointments and vacations and things to look forward to. An empty calendar forces you to make decisions on the spot.

One tip when booking appointments is to always book them as early as possible. This gives you something to look forward to when starting your day, and it gets you up in the morning. Planning ahead builds motivation.

I have a great tool you can download called the Daily Sales Planner Tool. You can write your daily goals, your personal goals, your appointments, your to-do list, and an end-of-day checklist. This is a simple planner tool that can help you stay focused and motivated. Download the planner here: SixFigureSalesAcademy.com/planner.

Another tool you can use is the rep Friday checklist. It gives you a checklist to go through to make sure you are fully prepared for the following week.

- Do you have appointments booked up for Monday–Wednesday?

- Do you have appointments booked out for the following week?

- Is your desk clean and organized?

- Is your car clean if you are a rep?

- Is your laptop/briefcase/backpack organized and admin work finished?

Before Friday ends, go through this checklist and make sure you are set for the next week. Think how powerful that is for walking into your weekend, knowing you are set for a strong next week and can enjoy your days off.

PRO TIPS AND A FREE GIFT FOR YOU

If you want to know my basic routine, you can download a sample here:

SixFigureSalesAcademy.com/routine

It's absolutely free, and I hope it helps you create one that works specifically for you. Once you work out a routine, make sure that you stick with it for 3–4 weeks before you decide to make a change. Remember, you are what you repeatedly do.

SECTION ELEVEN

Living by the C.H.A.N. Code

We are what we repeatedly do. Excellence, then, is not an act, but a habit.

—Aristotle

As you might be able to tell, I like blueprints, lists, frameworks, and acronyms. So it probably will come as no surprise that I made an acronym out of the letters of my last name. Some may find that narcissistic, but the truth is, I have a terrible memory and need simple frameworks to help me remember things. I'm a simple person with a simple code that has served me well, and I hope it serves you well too. I call it the C.H.A.N. Code. These are the four key principles that I live by. I'll give you examples of each, but in a nutshell, they are:

Cut the bullsh*t excuses.

Hustle daily.

Always get better.

Never ever give up.

C.H.A.N. CODE

C UT the bullsh*t excuses.

H USTLE daily.

A LWAYS get better.

N EVER give up.

Cut the bullsh*t excuses.

It was 2011. I was 26 years old, doing really well with my company. I was leading a 7-figure team and had gotten multiple promotions, broken lots of records, and gained loads of recognition. Life was going well. I had just bought my first house after getting married and finishing my MBA.

I was living the American dream and doing everything that I was expected to do, but I thought I wasn't tapping into my true potential. I wasn't sure if I could be this successful somewhere else.

So I made an educated decision to leave my company and go to a new company. It was two steps backward, but I was hoping it would lead to four or five steps forward. I remember everyone questioning and challenging me, "What are you doing? You have it so good. You're making such a great income."

I joined this new company, and I realized very quickly that I had joined the worst team in the worst region of the company.

No one believed they could make President's Club, there was high turnover, and it was a bad culture with people complaining nonstop.

They brought me in with a plan to sell for a couple of years, earn my stripes and show them how it is supposed to be done. They said, "If you do a really good job, we'll promote you to a sales leader role. Usually, it takes about three to five years to get promoted, but maybe you will get it in two years if you are lucky. But you'll still make a great income in the meantime."

I came in as a rookie and worked my butt off, especially for the first 8 or 9 weeks of rookie training, and I began getting results. People were noticing that I was doing a good job, especially being a rookie with the company, but I was disappointed. The bad culture and all the complaining were getting in my head.

I went to my boss, Travis, who was a great leader, and I said, "I don't know if I made the best decision coming here. Nobody knows me here. I came from a $20 billion company and people knew me. I'm a nobody here and I have to re-earn my stripes. I don't know if this is for me."

He asked, "Are you quitting?"

I replied, "No, I'm not quitting right now, but this isn't what I thought it would be. I'm just not happy."

He pulled up the leaderboard, looked me in the eye, and said, "Marcus, if you were number 1 right now, would that change how you are feeling?"

"Yeah, obviously."

"So you have to cut the bullshit. It's none of the things that you just told me, is it? You're just pissed you're not number 1."

And he was right. He called me on my bullshit. He pulled up a different report: a report that had all the rookie sales from the first 12 weeks. And I was crushing everyone. I just didn't have the perspective. I was caught up in my own bullshit, comparing myself to people who had been in this role for years with more pipeline and territory. Even though I was doing great for a rookie, I couldn't see through my bullshit, so he helped me to see that, which was so very powerful.

Fast forward, I stayed on top, crushing it. Within 9 months I became the sales manager—one of the fastest promotions to this title in the company's history.

If you want to achieve massive success in sales and life, drop the excuses and take ownership.

Hustle daily.

I was a new sales director in our Portland office. I had about 85 employees at the time, and I was always very transparent with my schedule. Even as a sales manager, I would post my schedule so everyone would know exactly where I was and who I was with at all times.

I did the same thing in this newly promoted role. I would travel Tuesday through Thursday with my days stacked from 5 a.m. to 10 p.m. each day. And then every Monday and Friday I would have 10–12 individual calls with my leaders going from 7 a.m. to 5 p.m. My calendar was packed to the brim and every minute was planned out.

On a Friday afternoon at about 4:30 p.m., it was just me and one of my newer reps left in the office.

He was getting ready to leave and knocked on my door. "Hey Marcus, how's it going?"

"Hey, it's great. Come on in and let's chat. How's everything going?"

He replied, "It's going great. It's hard, but I'm learning a lot. But I have to ask you a question. Why are you still here at 4:30 on a Friday afternoon? I see you here literally every Friday till after I leave. Why are you working so hard?"

I gave him a puzzled look. I couldn't comprehend his question. He added, "People at the same level as you are cutting out early, but you are always the last one here on Friday afternoons."

I laughed and replied, "Hey man, what got me here won't keep me here. It's relatively easy to get six-pack abs, but it's hard to keep them. Anyone can win one time, but being consistent takes work."

"Just because I got here, it's not about the destination. It's really about the journey and who I become. So I show up daily because every day I have to earn my keep. I have to show up today because tomorrow is never given. I have to earn it every single day. I work hard and smart. Just because I won President's Club and other awards in the past, it doesn't mean that I am going to do the same thing in this role. So I have to show that I can do it as well. I need to earn my stripes and prove to everyone that I can do it. But more importantly, I need to prove it to myself," I said.

I never changed my routine, and that year and every single year afterward, we hit President's Club and broke more and more records.

As JJ Watt says, "Success isn't owned, it's leased, and the rent is due every day." Continue to put in the work to earn it daily, no matter how successful you become.

Always get better.

As a sales director, I typically didn't run sales calls anymore except for the really big accounts where I would help to move the needle, close the deal, and support my reps.

But one of the things I did every week was to get into the field with a rep.

There were a few reasons why I did this. First, it helped keep me on top of my game. I could be sure that I stayed sharp in the field by doing what I would preach to my reps and keeping a consistent pulse on the customer.

The really cool part was that as I rode around with different reps, I would learn from each of them. It might be how they were organized, how they asked a question, how they phrased something, or how they used their body language to leverage the call. I could then internalize it and share it as a best practice across the board.

I would host a group call for each business unit every week and I would pick top performers to share their best practices as well. So this way, we could glean their knowledge, and it would enrich me as well because it's easy to get blinded by what you do.

I've always seen sales as a journey, and I want to keep learning and growing. The toughest people to sell to are always sales reps, especially when I am trying to train them. When I would come into an office to go on the field ride, I would also spend time in the office teaching them some specific tactics or sales strategies, and then I would role-play with them.

I always picked the people that I knew would try to bust my chops. I wanted everyone to see a tough prospect live. This not only made me better by picking the toughest opponent, but they would try to change the story and they would watch me navigate and dance around to handle whatever strategy I was trying to teach them.

Once I started my own business, I kept challenging myself. For every sales call I ran, I would listen to my own recording. I would evaluate it for how I opened the call, how I controlled it, the questions I would ask, the tonality, pace, and inflection, and I would gauge how they would respond. Then I would have a tight feedback loop so I could adjust for the next call.

This helped me improve my own sales process. Even though I have been in sales for years, I was now selling my own product, and I learned how to adapt it so I could have the highest optimal close rate.

Even to this day with my sales team, we listen to call recordings every week so we can get better and improve.

Humble yourself to learn and get better. Be willing to constantly learn and examine how other people are doing things and how you can improve.

Never ever give up.

I was in college, attending an event with a free buffet line. As a college kid, if it was free, I was there.

I was with my buddies, hanging out, having a good time, when I looked across the room filled with hundreds of people and there she was ... an incredibly gorgeous girl that I just had to meet.

Being a cocky, arrogant 19-year-old, I said to my friends, "Ok, guys. Watch this. I'm going to go get her number."

My friends shook their heads and watched as I approached this really hot girl, who proceeded to shut me down in front of everyone! I walked back like a puppy dog with its tail between its legs. My buddies were rolling on the floor laughing.

"Ok, haha, you guys are a bunch of clowns. But just wait, before we leave I'm going to get her number."

I went back and this time she gave it to me. I was so excited.

But over THE NEXT YEAR, I attempted to call and text her repeatedly ... with no response. Completely ghosted.

A year later, I ran into her at an event and she was really nice to me, but I was dating someone else. Fast forward *another* year later, I see her at the same fundraising event. And again, I'm dating someone else, so nothing happened.

Now skip ahead to summer 2006. I'm working for my parents at their restaurant. We had a booth selling Chinese food at a Scandinavian food festival. So I'm dressed up in a Scandinavian outfit. I had just gotten a new phone with a new number, so I was transferring all my data.

I came across an entry for "Sara Mo—hot Persian." I decided to text her: Hey, how's it going?

And she CALLS me back! I'm cooking hot noodles dressed in a Scandinavian costume three years after I first saw her, and she picks now to actually pick up the phone.

I answer. "Hello?"

She says, "Hi, who is this?" My heart drops. She doesn't know who I am.

"Hi, this is Marcus Chan."

"Oh, hi." I could hear a shift in her tonality. She didn't know who was calling her, and I'm not sure she remembered me.

She said she was moving back to Eugene, Oregon, where we had been going to school. I asked her if she needed help moving. Anyway, she didn't call me back to get help, but she did call me the next day and asked if I wanted to go get some coffee or ice cream.

I picked her up and we went out, and that's when I fell in love with her. Besides being beautiful, she was crazy smart, spoke five languages, and was just perfect.

We became great friends and started hanging out together every day. We would go to the library, study, and do home-work together. We were both trying to graduate and be done with school.

But I wanted to be more than friends. Over the next several months, we started kind of dating, but she wasn't willing to call me her boyfriend.

But I knew, beyond a shadow of a doubt, that I was going to marry this girl. It was unwavering faith. I'm not sure that she thought I was serious, so it took time.

But I was committed. I loved her and wanted it to be forever. So I played the long game and finally, after a whole other set of events (which is a story in and of itself), I proposed to her in front of her whole family ... and she said yes!

Over a decade later, I can tell you that I am thankful every single day for this amazing woman in my life.

Bottom line? When you really, truly desire something, never, ever give up. If you don't give up, you can never lose. For those who stay in the game, success is inevitable.

SECTION TWELVE

How to Get More Help

---

*It's good to learn from your mistakes. It's better
to learn from other people's mistakes.*
—Warren Buffett

How to Access Your Bonuses

How I Made $125,861 ($83,861 in Commissions and Bonuses) in a Brand New B2B Sales Role With Zero Pipeline

This 90-minute training covers how to maximize your sales income as fast as legally possible. This training covers many strategies mentioned in this book and shows you how to implement them effectively.

SixFigureSalesAcademy.com/win

Needs Assessment Discovery Worksheet

In this short training, we expand on how to map out your POWERFUL discovery questions using our simple downloadable Needs Assessment Discovery Worksheet.

SixFigureSalesAcademy.com/discovery

Goal Setting Worksheet

Setting clear goals is the first step toward achieving them. Use our simple Goal Setting Worksheet to plan out your goals. Head below to watch this bonus training and to grab the download.

SixFiguresalesAcademy.com/goals

Discovery Call Planning Sheet

The separation is in the preparation. In this bonus training, I break down exactly how to use the customizable Discovery Call Planning Sheet so you can walk into every sales call looking like a pro.

SixFigureSalesAcademy.com/prep

How to Create a Bulletproof 6- to 7-Figure Routine Worksheet

Having goals is the first step, but goals are only achieved if you have the right habits and routines. Watch this short bonus training and access the download on exactly how to create your Bulletproof 6- to 7-Figure+ Routine.

SixFigureSalesAcademy.com/routine

How to Create Your Own 6-Figure Friday Checklist

When done properly, your Fridays can become your most PROFITABLE days. Access this bonus training on how to use my 6-Figure Friday Checklist to set up your week for success.

SixFigureSalesAcademy.com/checklist

How to Plan Your Day Like a Top 1% Sales Pro

Staying organized is key to success, especially when planning for your day ahead. Watch this bonus training and access the Daily Sales Planner to help win your day.

SixFigureSalesAcademy.com/planner

Case Study

This is a video interview with one of our clients telling his story on how he went from earning $120K/year to $250K/year and in the Top 1% out of 600+ reps.

SixFigureSalesAcademy.com/reed

Client Results

If you are curious about what kind of results one can expect from implementing our strategies, I've compiled some screenshots from just a few of our premium clients, celebrating their wins. Feel free to check these out to inspire you toward what's possible.

SixFigureSalesAcademy.com/reviews

Next Steps to Help You Sell and Earn More

If you found this helpful and you want access to 30+ hours of killer FREE sales training and content to help you sell and earn more, subscribe to our YouTube channel below!

Inside you'll have access to trainings such as:

- The 30-Second Cold Video Message that has generated millions

- How to run discovery calls with a 30%+ closing ratio for $3K-$5M+ ARR deals

- The simple 5-Step Process that CRUSHES closing objections without feeling sleazy

- And tons more, along with future trainings too!

YouTube.com/c/MarcusChanimal

SPEAK TO US

If you're excited about what you've learned and would like some help from me and my team to implement all of the tactics and strategies ...

If you are a B2B sales professional who is looking to sell more and earn more—right now ...

We'd like to invite you to apply to work with us.

All you have to do is go to:

SixFigureSalesAcademy.com/go

On that page, you will see a calendar with a list of available dates and times for your call. Pick the one that works best for you and answer a few short questions about your situation and goals.

Once you have booked your time, you'll get to a page with instructions that explain how to prepare for your call. **Make sure to watch the video that walks you through what it's like to work with us.** Also, check out the case study so you'll get a practical example!

On the call, we will discuss your individual situation. If it looks like we can help, we will share exactly what it takes to work with us.

There's no obligation to join our coaching.

It's up to you to decide whether or not it's a good fit.

Visit **SixFigureSalesAcademy.com/go** to book your call today.

AFTERWORD

"You're working too hard," I said.

My new rep looked at me surprised. "Huh? What do you mean?"

I could understand why he was surprised. He was closing 3–4 accounts per week, which was over double what the average rep was doing.

I pulled his account list up and asked him, "See any common trends?"

He stared at the list and looked confused.

I started explaining, "Your average deal size is less than a third the size of our team's average account size, and all the businesses you've closed are very small local businesses doing barely $1M/year in sales at best.

If you simply dive deeper into the discovery and present larger solutions, you'll automatically increase your account size 3–5X without doing more work. And if you target larger businesses, you'll simply sell way larger deals too."

He started sputtering, "Well, these small businesses can't afford to spend more on our services! Especially not 3–5X more …"

I looked him straight in the eyes and said, "Did they tell you that? What makes you think they would be unwilling to pay more to get our top-tier solutions to solve their problems?"

He looked down. "Well, no ... I guess I personally wouldn't spend that much if I was them, but I guess I'm pretty cheap with stuff like this."

"Just because you're frugal, does that mean your prospects are as well?"

I saw the realization hit him.

The reality that we as salespeople SELL how we BUY.

That whatever we naturally value is how we then portray value to the prospect.

My rep was very frugal in his personal life. Anywhere he could save a penny, he would.

For instance, he loved to go to police auctions to buy BMWs, Mercedes, and other cars for a fraction of the dealership price. The cars would have all types of major issues but he would then spend all his weekends fixing them up as much as possible.

The cars might have looked nice on the outside but were filled with problems under the hood. But since they were way cheaper, he'd buy purely on price.

As a result, when he sold to prospects, he sold on price and not value. He would only present the lowest tier solutions as that is what he felt the most comfortable with, even if that was not the best solution for the prospect.

Selling the cheapest packages most aligned with his identity and was the most comfortable for him, so he naturally leaned into that without even realizing it.

Plus, it was easier to sell based on price as that takes virtually no sales skills, and you're essentially just an order-taker.

Selling based on value takes a lot of sales skills, and my rep was uncomfortable diving deep into the discovery phase and navigating the sales process. This explained why he also felt uncomfortable going after large enterprise organizations and selling multiple 6- to 7-figure opportunities.

My rep looked at me, "But you're pretty frugal. How are you able to sell the top-tier packages and 7-figure deals?"

I laughed and explained, "If there is something that I need but I don't see it to be of high value, I'll buy the cheapest option. For instance, I'll usually buy economy seats on short flights as I don't see the value in flying first class for a two-hour flight. But if it's something I see value in, I'll invest and pay more. For example, I spent $2,500 on a laptop as it can process more, which will save me time, and I can use the laptop to make more money."

I saw the lightbulb moment in my rep's eyes.

I continued.

"Thus, because I believe in value, I have zero issues selling a $250,000 contract to a prospect as I know it will save them hundreds of thousands of dollars in direct and indirect costs, while helping them generate millions of dollars.

It's a no-brainer in my mind, and it's my duty to help them solve their problem with the best possible solution. They can hear it in my tone, conviction, attitude … EVERYTHING."

It clicked.

Fast forward a few months as we continued working on his belief system and improving his sales skills, he started selling larger and larger solutions. He eventually also got more and more comfortable selling big solutions to bigger companies.

He worked less, was more effective, and had way better results.

He also ended up winning every single award every quarter and year, including President's Club. He earned multiple promotions and eventually even backfilled my role as the market manager.

And in his own personal life? Yup, he was now buying based on value for everything.

He was selling how he buys.

As I reflect back, it's funny how often this simple principle has shown up in my life.

For example, I remember having a conversation with a friend in January 2021. I had just completed my first full year in business as a solopreneur, and my friend was asking me how it went.

I could tell he was careful about asking as he knew most first-year businesses struggle a ton.

"Well, I was hoping to do $1M+ my first year but I fell short and only did a little over $650K."

My friend almost fell out of his chair. "How much??"

"It was actually $651,293, with one product under $10K. I was hoping for more, but I only had time for 10-15 hours/week for sales calls and the rest of the time was doing everything else in the business. That's why I'm hiring now."

My friend looked shocked and asked me how.

I explained that one of my favorite quotes is by Tony Robbins: "If you want to be successful, find someone who has achieved the results you want and copy what they do, and you'll achieve the same results."

I already knew there were others who had built wildly successful coaching businesses, so it made zero sense for me to reinvent the wheel.

Also, since time is my most valuable asset, I knew just trying to "YouTube it" and use trial and error would cost me far more in time and opportunity costs.

Plus, I wanted CONTEXT and not just content. I knew I needed the behind-the-scenes help for the fastest results as that is where the real magic is.

Therefore, I found a great business coach and invested $10K into their program.

I then took everything I learned from them and combined it with the sales skills that I had already honed over time.

I took the $10K and turned it into $651,293 in the first year alone.

And it's compounded exponentially every single year since then.

But the only way I was able to do that is because I sell how I buy.

I had no problem selling my program as I saw spending money as an investment.

It's exactly why I've invested over $250K into coaches, masterminds, and programs over the last decade.

And the return has been multiple 7-figures.

So if you're struggling to sell or you feel like you aren't reaching your full potential, you gotta ask yourself: Do you buy like you sell?

Just know there are better and faster ways to wild sales success.

Just do what I did. Find someone who has been wildly successful.

Then pay them whatever they want to show you EXACTLY how they do it.

Then take massive action.

The truth is sales can either be one of the highest paying jobs in the world, earning more than surgeons, doctors, and lawyers, or one of the lowest paying jobs in the world—depending on how good you are.

And you don't have to be born great at sales. You just have to acquire the skills to be great at it.

Remember: My start in sales was terrible, and I'm nobody special. In my heart, I'm still just that awkward, introverted

Asian kid who grew up dirt poor.

I've just learned that mastering sales is the fastest vehicle to a life of financial freedom, bulletproof confidence, and incredible achievements.

Not just for me, but for anyone in sales.

If I can do it, you can too.

The best investment you can make is an investment in yourself. The more you learn, the more you'll earn.

—Warren Buffett, Chairman and CEO
of Berkshire Hathaway
($95.9B Net Worth)

ACKNOWLEDGMENTS

I don't believe anyone is truly "self-made" as we all have received direct or indirect help, support, insight, and more from countless people.

I'll do my best to acknowledge as many as I can ...

I want to thank my wife, Sara Mostafavi, who has been with me through thick and thin as I learned the ropes to B2B sales, leadership, entrepreneurship, and more. I love you so much, and I would not have achieved a fraction of my success if it wasn't for your support.

I want to thank my son, Roman. Your creativity and passion for life inspire me to show up daily and to give 100%. I'm so proud of you and who you are becoming.

I want to thank my parents, Wai Yuen Chan and Ying Ying Hung. You both sacrificed everything to immigrate to America and then worked endlessly to give us the opportunity to write our own ticket. You pushed and challenged me as a kid, but you made me realize that we all have greatness within that is just waiting to be tapped.

I want to thank my sisters, Angela and Jennifer Chan, for putting up with me as kids and as adults. I know I'm quirky, but your support and love have always been there.

I want to thank my nieces and nephews, Koa Strom, Kyan Strom, Kavaun Gregory, and Roya Gregory. You four are growing up to be brilliant and beautiful human beings and I know you will each change the world.

I want to thank my in-laws, Mike Mostafavi and Haydeh Kiani. You welcomed me into your family with open and loving arms while providing me with undying support, even when I was just starting my career and was just a boy in love with your daughter.

I want to thank my sister and brother-in-law, Beata Mostafavi and Nick Gregory. You have been big supporters from day one and it is much appreciated.

I want to thank all the brilliant salespeople, sales leaders, and entrepreneurs that I have learned so much from over the years, whether it was directly or indirectly. The lessons I've learned and gathered over time have been key for my sales foundation, mindset, and more.

I want to thank my past employers and the leadership teams there as they gave me the opportunity to cut my teeth and learn how to sell effectively. I had several direct and indirect mentors there, and they all have had an influence on how I sell and who I've become.

I want to thank Joor Bol, one of my first sales hires. Your coachability and commitment to excellence were pivotal in helping me in a sales team rebuild that helped launch future success. I'm so proud of all that you've achieved professionally and personally.

As I'm a firm believer that I'll never "know it all" in sales, I want to thank Dan Henry for introducing me to the world of online sales funnels and how to build a business online.

I want to thank Ravi Abuvala for helping me learn how to effectively build systems to scale my business to the next level.

You helped me fill in the gaps in my business and have been instrumental in my company's growth.

I want to thank Ian Koniak for not just writing the foreword, but for your friendship and camaraderie. It's been amazing watching you build your business from scratch. Game respects game.

I want to thank Jason Bay and Kyle Vamvouris. I value our entrepreneur mastermind get-togethers. You two make me better.

I want to thank my team, especially Christian Parra, Shari Julagay, and Cloud Seballos. You saw the vision from the get-go and have been instrumental in helping grow the business. Your hard work and loyalty do not go unnoticed.

Special thanks to Shanda Trofe for helping me publish my first book. Without your direction and design, this would still be just an idea.

A huge thank you to Lori Lynn and your team—especially Mary Rembert for helping take the ideas in my head and making sure they were structured and edited properly, Clare Fernández for smoothing out transitions and creating design mockups, Linda Bourdeaux for designing the infographics, and Jessica Welch for the final proofreading polish. Because of you all, these concepts actually make sense. This book wouldn't be here without your help.

A big thank you to Tyler Wagner for helping me spread my message to as many people as possible. Your marketing genius is much appreciated.

Special thank you for the following amazing humans for taking the time to read the early versions and for helping me make this book world class: Jay Abbasi, Alex Alleyne, Jarrod Best-Mitchell, John Barrows, Paul Caffrey, Nick Capozzi, Ivan Dikiy, Kevin Dorsey, Jonathan Dunn, Robb Gilbear, Ray Green, Phil Jones, Niraj Kapur, Doug Lawson, Alex Newmann, Simon Parson, David Priemer, Ravi Rajani, Jamal Reimer, Alex Sheridan, Salina Yeung, Jeremy Bogard, Abner Castenada, Tim Chandler, Pierra Clemons, Draper Donley, Zachary Faerber, Brenda Fitzgerald, Justin Kenny, Ryan Kent, Joe Kivlin, Alan Leung, Iris Monterrosa, Kyle Morini, Chan Oh, Josh Patino, Dustin Phillips, Samantha Price, Lucas Schmeisl, LJ Stojanovski, Tanya Sherman, Abid Sikder, Brad Stout, and Nick Wiley.

Last, but not least, thank YOU for buying this book. For taking the time to read it and execute on the contents. You've shown you have what it takes to become elite at sales by simply investing in yourself to start!

ABOUT THE AUTHOR

Marcus Chan is the founder of Venli Consulting Group and Six-Figure Sales Academy, catering to an audience of more than 50,000 B2B sales professionals. He is a member of the Forbes Business Council and has been recognized globally as one of the top sales experts by Salesforce and LinkedIn.

An award-winning Fortune 500 sales leader who has generated over $700M in sales over the last decade, he has been featured in Forbes, Yahoo! Finance, MarketWatch, Entrepreneur, and more.

His sole mission is to help B2B sales pros and solopreneurs increase their income by an ADDITIONAL $50K–100K+/ year by running a refined sales process that gets results and helps them create the life of their dreams.

YOUR FREE TICKET

In addition to the short bonus training videos included in this book, I've created a special one-hour training for you that shows exactly how to outperform your competition so you can work fewer hours and make more sales.

If you learn better by seeing and hearing, you will love this training. It will take what you've learned in this book and cement the concepts so they become second nature.

I recommend watching the training from beginning to end first. Then, go back a second time to take notes. Immediately apply what you've learned to build your bulletproof sales mindset.

I can't guarantee how long the training will be there, so get it while it's hot:

SixFigureSalesAcademy.com/ticket

Printed in Great Britain
by Amazon

86361180R00145